SCIENCE IN A GARDEN

Activities and projects for the outdoor classroom,

Years F-6

Ross Mars

To all of my children and grandchildren,
who make my life complete

© 2023 Ross Mars

All rights reserved. No part of this book may be reproduced or transmitted in any form or by any means, electronic or mechanical, including photocopying, recording or by any information storage and retrieval system, without prior permission in writing from the publisher.

Published in 2023 by Amba Press, Melbourne, Australia.
www.ambapress.com.au

Access the resources, templates and reproducibles from the book at
www.ambapress.com.au/products/science-in-a-garden

Previously published in 2021 by Hawker Brownlow Education.

This edition replaces all previous editions.

ISBN: 9781923116184 (pbk)
ISBN: 9781923116207 (ebk)

A catalogue record for this book is available from the National Library of Australia.

Illustrations by Brenna Quinlan and Simone Willis.

Recipes on pages 177–178 and 187–189 first appeared in the book *How to permaculture your life* (2015) by Ross Mars and Simone Willis. They are reproduced here with permission.

ACKNOWLEDGEMENTS

My sincere thanks go to Brenna Quinlan and Simone Willis for their artwork and drawings, and to Jenny for her continued support and encouragement.

TABLE OF CONTENTS

About the author xi
Foreword xiii
Australian Curriculum links xv

Part 1: Understanding science in the garden 1

Teacher notes	Creating an outside garden classroom	2
Background	Understanding science in the garden	6
Background	Safety in the garden	11
Activity	Tools and their functions	14
Activity	Tools and tasks	17
Project	Science is observation	18
Activity	Exploring your garden	19
Activity	Shapes of leaves	23

Part 2: Growth in the garden 25

Teacher notes	Seed germination (Investigations 1 to 5)	26
Investigation	Germination 1: The effect of light on germination	28
Investigation	Germination 2: The effect of temperature on germination	30
Investigation	Germination 3: The effect of salt on germination	32
Investigation	Germination 4: The effect of smoke water on germination	35
Investigation	Germination 5: The effect of water on germination	37
Activity	Plant parts	40
Activity	Stages of plant growth	41
Teacher notes	Rate of plant growth	42
Investigation	Rate of plant growth	43
Project	Growth diary	45
Investigation	The life cycle of a flowering plant	50
Investigation	Transpiration	53
Investigation	Oxygen production	54
Investigation	Glucose production	55
Investigation	Starch	56

Part 3: Changes in the garden ... 57

Background	Seasons	58
Project	The seasonal calendar for First Australians	59
Background	Changes in the garden	60
Activity	Uses of deciduous trees	61
Activity	Seasonal changes in plants	62
Background	Water in the garden	63
Teacher notes	About water	64
Activity	What is so important about water?	65
Background	Water cycle processes	66
Investigation	The water cycle (in a bag)	67
Investigation	The water cycle (in a cup)	68
Investigation	How does water get clean?	70
Investigation	Movement of rain	72
Investigation	Cyclone in a jar	73
Investigation	Mixing materials: Water and oil	74
Investigation	Changes to soil temperature	76
Investigation	Causes of erosion	79

Part 4: Animals in the garden ... 81

Background	Needs and uses of animals	82
Activity	Needs and uses of animals	83
Activity	Animal products and functions	85
Activity	Animals in schools	86
Activity	What animal is that? bingo	88
Activity	Adaptations	92
Activity	Adaptations in garden animals	95
Teacher notes	Nocturnal animal adaptations	98
Background	Mouthpart adaptations in insects	102
Activity	How do these insects feed?	104
Investigation	Pollination	105
Activity	Pollination	106
Background	Adaptations in bees	108
Activity	Adaptations in bees	110
Activity	Australian native bees	111
Activity	Butterflies	112
Teacher notes	Adaptations in birds	113
Activity	Adaptations in birds	114

Teacher notes	Adaptations in common garden animal pests	116
Activity	Adaptations in common garden animal pests	118
Background	Predators in the garden	119
Activity	Predators in the garden	120
Activity	Your garden ecosystem	122
Background	Pest control	124
Activity	Soil critters	126

Part 5: Human use of the garden 129

Investigation	Bush medicine plants	130
Activity	Nutritional value of bush foods	132
Teacher notes	Growing a bush food and bush medicinal garden	135
Activity	First Australians and the environment	138
Teacher notes	Earth pigments	139
Project	Painting with earth pigments	140
Teacher notes	Grow your own clothes	141
Teacher notes	Weaving (fibre basketry)	145
Project	Make your own sundial	148
Activity	Minimising waste in the garden	150
Teacher notes	A waste audit	152
Investigation	A waste audit	153
Activity	Waste audit evaluation	156

Part 6: Products from the garden 157

Background	Food from the garden	158
Activity	Using food from the garden	159
Activity	Types of vegetables	160
Activity	Construct a food pyramid	162
Teacher notes	Moulds	164
Investigation	Growing mould	165
Investigation	What bread mould needs to grow	167
Teacher notes	Yeast (Investigations 1 to 3)	169
Investigation	Yeast 1: The action of yeast	171
Investigation	Yeast 2: Measuring gas production by yeast	173
Investigation	Yeast 3: Factors affecting the action of yeast	175
Project	Make sourdough bread	177
Project	Make spelt bread	179
Investigation	Gluten	181

Project	Make gluten-free bread	182
Project	Make damper bread	184
Background	Simple products to make from milk	186
Project	Food products from milk	187
Investigation	Make your own plastic from milk	190
Investigation	Make your own glues from milk	191
Project	Make your own honeycomb	192
Project	Herb sauces	195
Project	Classroom cookbook	199
Project	Make your own hand sanitiser spray	200
Project	Playdough garden decorations	202

Appendix 205

Answers	Tools and their functions	206
Answers	Plant parts	208
Answers	Stages of plant growth	209
Answers	Needs and uses of animals	210
Answers	How do these insects feed?	212
Answers	Pollination	213
Answers	Adaptations in birds	214
Answers	Soil critters	214
Answers	Nutritional value of bush foods	215
Answers	Using food from the garden	217
Answers	Types of vegetables	218

ABOUT THE AUTHOR

Dr Ross Mars began his career as a senior secondary school science teacher, writing and co-writing a number of books about science and technology.

Over the last twenty years, he has worked in the water industry, focusing on wastewater treatment and re-use. He has presented papers at a number of international conferences, both in Australia and overseas, and has had several papers published in scientific journals.

Ross is one of the most authoritative permaculture teachers, designers and consultants in Australia, authoring three books on the subject as well as other resources on energy-efficient housing design and renewable energy systems for power generation.

More recently, Ross has developed and introduced the new accredited permaculture courses in Western Australia, including Certificate I and Certificate II VET programs for schools and community groups as well as all courses up to the diploma level in permaculture.

Ross maintains a strong interest in preparing people for the transition to sustainable living, especially as we move into a challenging and uncertain future, and he continues to work as an educator and author.

FOREWORD

Letter for letter, sentence for sentence and paragraph for paragraph we are living in a world where information is cheap. It is everywhere. We are bombarded wherever we go with facts and figures. Most of us have a machine in our pocket that is rarely switched off, and it is overwhelming us with a non-stop feed. The real question is: Where do we go for credible information, experience, know-how and a proven track record that stands up in these times of saturation? Well, it seems that for all the technical development, reach and incredible accessibility that the worldwide web brings, a good (seemingly) old-fashioned three-dimensional book still holds a certain level of credibility given the time and resources spent producing such a physical item.

When it comes to environmental education there has not been a point in history where its importance has been more front and centre. But, naturally, it is competing in a media landscape that has many other priorities. During a year when the world has been forced to stop, shut down and reflect on the breakneck pace of growth and development, people have been seeing the world around them in a new light. Families and individuals have had time to look at the streets and parks and landscapes that make up their home and engage with nature in new and simple ways. They have had a chance to look at the garden planet they live in. People have asked questions of the spaces around them, begun gardening and growing and creating habitats and spaces for nature to return. However, in doing this, people have had questions that they want answers to. This is a generation that, when focused, requires information quickly, and they seek this information out rigorously. This makes the release of *Science in a garden* incredibly timely.

So, at a time when people want answers and information, Ross Mars is perfectly placed to oblige them. As an environmental educator and permaculturist, Ross has been delivering these answers for a long time, decades in fact. I first met Ross at a permaculture convergence in Kuranda, Far North Queensland, back in 2010. We locked horns immediately, bantering at every opportunity about the role of education in a changing world, and it was clear to see that his experience and scientific knowledge as an educator was the pillar on which he was taking responsibility for the challenges at hand. This is his passion, so you only need to look at the table of contents to see the detail and scope within which Ross works. The book is a brilliant mix of scientific facts and figures delivered through a range of activities and challenges that are designed to engage creative and inquisitive minds. And this is what makes the book such a valuable resource.

With so much information and, in many cases, depressing statistics about the state of the environment delivered daily in the news and online, *Science in a garden* is a positive elixir, a go-to reference book for teachers and students to find instruction that inspires investigation and understanding of the world around us. Teachers are constantly on the lookout for reference materials that challenge students, and I would go so far as to say also challenge them to see new ways of delivering morsels of timely information in a way that it creates the drive and desire to learn more. When scientific concepts are carefully and thoroughly explained, it helps give teachers ideas and inspirations to take their perspectives and share them in new ways. Clear, articulate and really well-illustrated by the talented Brenna Quinlan and Simone Willis, this book informs teachers and parents in such a way that they can easily support and provoke students to thrive and strive. What's more, by being linked to the Australian Curriculum, it ties the outcomes of the activities to students and their progress through the required stages of learning. Building this pedagogy of learning into our education system from primary school is a setting that will grow a legacy of significance around our students and their connection to country.

There has been great interest in and development of school gardens over the last 10 to 15 years, and it is common knowledge that the garden is an ideal outdoor classroom. *Science in a garden* is the perfect tool to help make the most of outdoor learning spaces by immersing students in nature through hands-on activity. And not just activity that ticks a box and fills the class time, not a nice distraction from the core learning. Far from it. Outdoor classes are the real deal, and Ross's valuable synthesis of facts and action helps validate the scope of learning across all disciplines. Contemporary science is a given, but the teaching and learning strategies recognising the foundational role that Indigenous and First Nations peoples' knowledge and learning plays in the context of the present is a recipe for reconciliation.

This book can be given not just to students and parents but equally as a valuable addition to every teacher's wheelbarrow of engagement. It is the result of years of time on the ground teaching, presenting and learning ever-evolving ways of creating yarns about life through many lenses. And what better way to prepare our next generation for the world they will inherit than with a kitbag of skills and ways of seeing and loving their world through understanding, responsibility and lifelong action?

Costa Georgiadis BLArch (UNSW)

AUSTRALIAN CURRICULUM LINKS

Australian Curriculum: Science, Foundation to Year 2

Level	Strands	Elaborations	Links
F	Living things have basic needs, including food and water (ACSSU002)	Recognising the needs of living things in a range of situations such as pets at home, plants in the garden or plants and animals in bushland	Germination 1–5 (p. 28) Needs and uses of animals (p. 83) What bread mould needs to grow (p. 167)
F	Science involves observing, asking questions about, and describing changes in, objects and events (ACSHE013)	Recognising that observation is an important part of exploring and investigating the things and places around us Sharing observations with others and communicating their experiences Exploring and observing using the senses: hearing, smell, touch, sight and taste	Science is observation (p. 18) Exploring your garden (p. 19) Shapes of leaves (p. 23) Exploring your garden (p. 19) Playdough garden decorations (p. 202)
F	Participate in guided investigations and make observations using the senses (ACSIS011)	Using sight, hearing, touch, taste and smell so that students can gather information about the world around them	Exploring your garden (p. 19) Simple products to make from milk (p. 186)
F	Engage in discussions about observations and represent ideas (ACSIS233)	Taking part in informal and guided discussions relating to students' observations Using drawings to represent observations and ideas and discussing their representations with others	Shapes of leaves (p. 23) Plant parts (p. 40) Stages of plant growth (p. 41) Rate of plant growth (p. 43) Growth diary (p. 45) Your garden ecosystem (p. 122)
F	Share observations and ideas (ACSIS012)	Working in groups to describe what students have done and what they have found out Communicating ideas through role play and drawing	Exploring your garden (p. 19) Shapes of leaves (p. 23) Growth diary (p. 45) Water cycle processes (p. 66) Food from the garden (p. 158) Playdough garden decorations (p. 202)
1	Living things have a variety of external features (ACSSU017)	Identifying common features of plants such as leaves and roots Describing the use of plant parts for particular purposes such as making food and obtaining water	Plant parts (p. 40) Types of vegetables (p. 160)

continued

Level	Strands	Elaborations	Links
1	Living things live in different places where their needs are met (ACSSU211)	Recognising that different living things live in different places such as land and water	Exploring your garden (p. 19) Needs and uses of animals (p. 83) Adaptations in garden animals (p. 95) Adaptations in birds (p. 114) Your garden ecosystem (p. 122)
1	Everyday materials can be physically changed in a variety of ways (ACSSU018)	Exploring how materials such as water, chocolate or playdough change when warmed or cooled	The water cycle (in a bag) (p. 67) The water cycle (in a cup) (p. 68) Simple products to make from milk (p. 186) Make your own honeycomb (p. 192) Herb sauces (p. 195) Classroom cookbook (p. 199) Playdough garden decorations (p. 202)
1	Science involves observing, asking questions about, and describing changes in, objects and events (ACSHE021)	Jointly constructing questions about the events and features of the local environment with teacher guidance	Exploring your garden (p. 19) Rate of plant growth (p. 43)
1	People use science in their daily lives, including when caring for their environment and living things (ACSHE022)	Considering how science is used in activities such as cooking, fishing, transport, sport, medicine and caring for plants and animals	Yeast 1–3 (p. 171) Simple products to make from milk (p. 186) Make sourdough bread (p. 188)
1	Use informal measurements to collect and record observations, using digital technologies as appropriate (ACSIS026)	Using units that are familiar to students from home and school, such as cups (cooking), hand spans (length) and walking paces (distance) to make and record observations with teacher guidance	Make spelt bread (p. 179) Simple products to make from milk (p. 186) Make your own hand sanitiser spray (p. 200)
1	Represent and communicate observations and ideas in a variety of ways (ACSIS029)	Discussing or representing what was discovered in an investigation Engaging in whole class or guided small group discussions to share observations and ideas	Safety in the garden (p. 11) Tools and their functions (p. 14) Tools and tasks (p. 17) Water in the garden (p. 63) Water cycle processes (p. 66)
2	Different materials can be combined for a particular purpose (ACSSU031)	Exploring the local environment to observe a variety of materials, and describing ways in which materials are used Investigating the effects of mixing materials together	Exploring your garden (p. 19) Mixing materials: Water and oil (p. 74) Simple products to make from milk (p. 186) Make your own honeycomb (p. 192) Herb sauces (p. 195) Classroom cookbook (p. 199)

continued

Level	Strands	Elaborations	Links
2	Earth's resources are used in a variety of ways (ACSSU032)	Identifying the Earth's resources including water, soil and minerals, and describing how they are used in the school	What is so important about water? (p. 65) How does water get clean? (p. 70) Causes of erosion (p. 79)
2	Science involves observing, asking questions about, and describing changes in, objects and events (ACSHE034)	Identifying and describing sources of water	Water cycle processes (p. 66) The water cycle (in a bag) (p. 67) The water cycle (in a cup) (p. 68) How does water get clean? (p. 70) Movement of rain (p. 72) Cyclone in a jar (p. 73) Causes of erosion (p. 79)
2	People use science in their daily lives, including when caring for their environment and living things (ACSHE035)	Investigating how Aboriginal and Torres Strait Islander Peoples use science to meet their needs, such as food supply Identifying the ways humans manage and protect resources, such as reducing waste and caring for water supplies	The seasonal calendar for first Australians (p. 59) What is so important about water? (p. 65) Bush medicine plants (p. 130) Nutritional value of bush foods (p. 132) Growing a bush food and bush medicinal garden (p. 135) First Australians and the environment (p. 138) Painting with earth pigments (p. 140) Weaving (fibre basketry) (p. 145) Minimising waste in the garden (p. 150) A waste audit (p. 153) Waste audit evaluation (p. 156)
2	Pose and respond to questions, and make predictions about familiar objects and events (ACSIS037)	Using the senses to explore the local environment to pose interesting questions, make inferences and predictions	Exploring your garden (p. 19)
2	Participate in guided investigations to explore and answer questions (ACSIS038)	Manipulating objects and materials and making observations of the results	Movement of rain (p. 72) Cyclone in a jar (p. 73) Simple products to make from milk (p. 186) Playdough garden decorations (p. 202)
2	Use informal measurements to collect and record observations, using digital technologies as appropriate (ACSIS039)	Using units that are familiar to students from home and school, such as cups (cooking), hand spans (length) and walking paces (distance) to make and compare observations	Make sourdough bread (p. 177) Make damper bread (p. 184) Simple products to make from milk (p. 186) Herb sauces (p. 195) Classroom cookbook (p. 199)

continued

Level	Strands	Elaborations	Links
2	Represent and communicate observations and ideas in a variety of ways (ACSIS042)	Presenting ideas to other students, both one-to-one and in small groups Discussing with others what was discovered from an investigation	Water cycle processes (p. 66) Mixing materials: Water and oil (p. 74) Needs and uses of animals (p. 83) Simple products to make from milk (p. 186)

Australian Curriculum: Technologies, Foundation to Year 2

Level	Strands	Elaborations	Links
F–2	Identify how people design and produce familiar products, services and environments and consider sustainability to meet personal and local community needs (ACTDEK001)	Asking questions about natural and managed environments and impacts on them when selecting materials, tools and equipment when designing and making products, for example harvesting products from the school garden and using recycled clothing Making design decisions based on personal and family needs, for example downloading and comparing recipes to suit available cooking facilities such as cooking in the bush compared to cooking in a kitchen Exploring and critiquing products, services and environments for their impact on sustainability, for example the environmental risks and benefits of a system for organically or hydroponically growing a vegetable crop from seed or seedling to harvest	Tools and their functions (p. 14) Tools and tasks (p. 17) Construct a food pyramid (p. 162) Make damper bread (p. 184) Simple products to make from milk (p. 186) Classroom cookbook (p. 199)

continued

Level	Strands	Elaborations	Links
F–2	Explore how plants and animals are grown for food, clothing and shelter and how food is selected and prepared for healthy eating (ACTDEK003)	Exploring which plants and animals can provide food or materials for clothing and shelter and what basic needs those plants and animals have	Needs and uses of animals (p. 83) Grow your own clothes (p. 141)
		Identifying products that can be designed and produced from plants and animals, for example food products, paper and wood products, fabrics and yarns, and fertilisers	Animal products and functions (p. 85) Weaving (fibre basketry) (p. 145) Types of vegetables (p. 160) Simple products to make from milk (p. 186)
		Considering the suitability of a range of tools when cultivating gardens, mulching and building garden structures and preparing and cooking food from recipes	Safety in the garden (p. 11) Tools and their functions (p. 14) Tools and tasks (p. 17) Make gluten-free bread (p. 182)
		Identifying and categorising a wide range of foods, including Aboriginal bush foods, into food groups and describing tools and equipment needed to prepare these for healthy eating	Nutritional value of bush foods (p. 132) Construct a food pyramid (p. 162)
		Exploring how people from different cultures, including those of Asia, design and produce different cuisines based on the plants and animals in their region and available tools and equipment	Construct a food pyramid (p. 162) Simple products to make from milk (p. 186)
		Exploring the tools, equipment and techniques used to prepare food safely and hygienically for healthy eating	Using food from the garden (p. 59) Make sourdough bread (p. 177) Make gluten-free bread (p. 182) Simple products to make from milk (p. 186)
F–2	Explore needs or opportunities for designing, and the technologies needed to realise designed solutions (ACTDEP005)	Exploring opportunities around the school for designing solutions, for example how school play areas could be improved; how the school removes classroom waste and identifying opportunities to reduce, recycle and re-use materials; reviewing the school canteen menu to identify healthy food options and suggesting changes to promote future good health	Exploring your garden (p. 19) Minimising waste in the garden (p. 150) A waste audit (p. 153) Waste audit evaluation (p. 156) Construct a food pyramid (p. 162) Herb sauces (p. 195) Classroom cookbook (p. 199)
		Exploring which tools, equipment and techniques to use with selected materials	Safety in the garden (p. 11) Tools and their functions (p. 14) Tools and tasks (p. 17) Using food from the garden (p. 159)

continued

Level	Strands	Elaborations	Links
F–2	Generate, develop and record design ideas through describing, drawing and modelling (ACTDEP006)	Identifying one common testing method, and recording results, for example taste-testing comparisons of a food product and recording results in a digital form	Make sourdough bread (p. 177) Make damper bread (p. 184) Simple products to make from milk (p. 186)
F–2	Use materials, components, tools, equipment and techniques to safely make designed solutions (ACTDEP007)	Learning and safely practising a range of technical skills using tools and equipment, for example joining techniques when making products, watering and mulching gardens, preparing food, using software to design an environment	Tools and their functions (p. 14) Tools and tasks (p. 17) Using food from the garden (p. 159)
F–2	Use personal preferences to evaluate the success of design ideas, processes and solutions including their care for environment (ACTDEP008)	Reflecting on the processes and challenges of designing and producing a solution and sharing these reflections using digital technologies, for example when growing a food product, designing a structure to take a load or making a nutritious snack	Rate of plant growth (p. 43) Growth diary (p. 45) Grow your own clothes (p. 141) Make your own sundial (p. 148)
F–2	Sequence steps for making designed solutions and working collaboratively (ACTDEP009)	Recording the procedure for making a product, for example a recipe or instructions for making a container Identifying roles for each member of a group when working collaboratively	Make your own sundial (p. 148) Simple products to make from milk (p. 186) Classroom cookbook (p. 199) Simple products to make from milk (p. 186) Make your own hand sanitiser spray (p. 200)

Australian Curriculum: Science, Years 3 to 4

Level	Strands	Elaborations	Links
3	With guidance, identify questions in familiar contexts that can be investigated scientifically and make predictions based on prior knowledge (ACSIS053)	Choosing questions to investigate from a list of possibilities Jointly constructing questions that may form the basis for investigation Listing shared experiences as a whole class and identifying possible investigations Working in groups to discuss things that might happen during an investigation	Germination 1–5 (p. 28) Yeast 1–3 (p. 171)
3	With guidance, plan and conduct scientific investigations to find answers to questions, considering the safe use of appropriate materials and equipment (ACSIS054)	Working with teacher guidance to plan investigations to test simple cause-and-effect relationships Discussing as a whole class ways to investigate questions and evaluating which ways might be most successful	Mixing materials: Water and oil (p. 74) Germination 1–5 (p. 28)
3	Use a range of methods including tables and simple column graphs to represent data and to identify patterns and trends (ACSIS057)	Discussing how to graph data presented in a table Identifying and discussing numerical and visual patterns in data collected from students' own investigations and from secondary sources	Rate of plant growth (p. 43) The life cycle of a flowering plant (p. 50) Changes to soil temperature (p. 76)
3	Represent and communicate observations, ideas and findings using formal and informal representations (ACSIS060)	Communicating with other students carrying out similar investigations to share experiences and improve investigation skill Exploring different ways to show processes and relationships through diagrams, models and role play Using simple explanations and arguments, reports or graphical representations to communicate ideas to other students	The life cycle of a flowering plant (p. 50) Changes to soil temperature (p. 76)
4	Living things have life cycles (ACSSU072)	Making and recording observations of living things as they develop through their life cycles Describing the stages of life cycles of different living things such as insects, birds, frogs and flowering plants	The life cycle of a flowering plant (p. 50) Changes in the garden (p. 60) Uses of deciduous trees (p. 61) Seasonal changes in plants (p. 62)
4	Living things depend on each other and the environment to survive (ACSSU073)	Investigating how plants provide shelter for animals Investigating the roles of living things in a habitat, for instance producers, consumers or decomposers	Needs and uses of animals (p. 83) Predators in the garden (p. 120) Your garden ecosystem (p. 122) Soil critters (p. 126)

continued

Level	Strands	Elaborations	Links
4	Natural and processed materials have a range of physical properties that can influence their use (ACSSU074)	Describing a range of common materials, such as metals or plastics, and their uses	Make your own sundial (p. 148) Minimising waste in the garden (p. 150) Waste audit evaluation (p. 156) Playdough garden decorations (p. 202)
4	Earth's surface changes over time as a result of natural processes and human activity (ACSSU075)	Investigating the characteristics of soils	Causes of erosion (p. 79) Soil critters (p. 126)
4	Science knowledge helps people to understand the effect of their actions (ACSHE062)	Considering methods of waste management and how they can affect the environment	Minimising waste in the garden (p. 150) A waste audit (p. 153) Waste audit evaluation (p. 156)
4	With guidance, identify questions in familiar contexts that can be investigated scientifically and make predictions based on prior knowledge (ACSIS064)	Reflecting on familiar situations to make predictions with teacher guidance	Germination 1–5 (p. 28) Yeast 1–3 (p. 171)
4	With guidance, plan and conduct scientific investigations to find answers to questions, considering the safe use of appropriate materials and equipment (ACSIS065)	Exploring different ways to conduct investigations and connecting these to the types of questions asked with teacher guidance Working in groups, with teacher guidance, to plan ways to investigate questions Discussing and recording safety rules for equipment as a whole class	Safety in the garden (p. 11) Germination 1–5 (p. 28) Using food from the garden (p. 159) Yeast 1–3 (p. 171)
4	Consider the elements of fair tests and use formal measurements and digital technologies as appropriate, to make and record observations accurately (ACSIS066)	Making and recording measurements using familiar formal units and appropriate abbreviations, such as seconds (s), grams (g), centimetres (cm) and millilitres (mL) Recognising the elements of a fair test and using these when planning the steps and processes of an investigation	Germination 1–5 (p. 28) Nutritional value of bush foods (p. 132) Yeast 1–3 (p. 171)
4	Use a range of methods including tables and simple column graphs to represent data and to identify patterns and trends (ACSIS068)	Identifying and discussing numerical and visual patterns in data collected from students' investigations and from other sources Discussing with teacher guidance which graphic organisers will be most useful in sorting or organising data arising from investigations	The life cycle of a flowering plant (p. 50) Changes to soil temperature (p. 76) Germination 1–5 (p. 28) Yeast 1–3 (p. 171)

continued

Level	Strands	Elaborations	Links
4	Reflect on investigations, including whether a test was fair or not (ACSIS069)	Reflecting on investigations, identifying what went well, what was difficult or didn't work so well, and how well the investigation helped answer the question	Germination 1–5 (p. 28) Changes to soil temperature (p. 76) Yeast 1–3 (p. 171)
4	Compare results with predictions, suggesting possible reasons for findings (ACSIS216)	Discussing how well predictions matched results from an investigation and proposing reasons for findings Comparing, in small groups, proposed reasons for findings and explaining their reasoning	Germination 1–5 (p. 28) Yeast 1–3 (p. 171)
4	Represent and communicate observations, ideas and findings using formal and informal representations (ACSIS071)	Communicating with other students carrying out similar investigations to share experiences and improve investigation skills Using simple explanations and arguments, reports or graphical representations to communicate ideas to other students	Germination 3 (p. 32) The life cycle of a flowering plant (p. 50) Changes to soil temperature (p. 76) What bread mould needs to grow (p. 167)

Australian Curriculum: Technologies, Years 3 to 4

Level	Strands	Elaborations	Links
3–4	Recognise the role of people in design and technologies occupations and explore factors, including sustainability that impact on the design of products, services and environments to meet community needs (ACTDEK010)	Considering the impact of environments on users, for example a school vegetable garden, a protected outdoor play area	Exploring your garden (p. 19) First Australians and the environment (p. 138) Painting with earth pigments (p. 140) Using food from the garden (p. 159) Construct a food pyramid (p. 162)
3–4	Investigate food and fibre production and food technologies used in modern and traditional societies (ACTDEK012)	Exploring tools, equipment and procedures to improve plant and animal production, for example when growing vegetables in the school garden and producing plant and animal environments such as a greenhouse, animal housing, safe bird shelters Describing ideal conditions for successful plant and animal production including how climate and soils affect production and availability of foods, for example Aboriginal seasons and food availability	Exploring you garden (p. 19) The seasonal calendar for First Australian (p. 59) Needs and uses of animals (p. 83) Bush medicine plants (p. 130) First Australians and the environment (p. 138) Weaving (fibre basketry) (p. 145) Using food from the garden (p. 159) Classroom cookbook (p. 199)

continued

Level	Strands	Elaborations	Links
3–4	Investigate the suitability of materials, systems, components, tools and equipment for a range of purposes (ACTDEK013)	Investigating the suitability of technologies – materials, systems, components, tools and equipment – when designing and making a product, service or environment, for example a toy for a young child, a composting system for household waste management, raised garden beds for improved access, weaving nets, bags or baskets	Painting with earth pigments (p. 140) Weaving (fibre basketry) (p. 145) Make your own sundial (p. 148) Waste audit evaluation (p. 156) Using food from the garden (p. 159) Simple products to make from milk (p. 186) Classroom cookbook (p. 199)
3–4	Select and use materials, components, tools, equipment and techniques and use safe work practices to make designed solutions (ACTDEP016)	Using tools and equipment accurately when measuring, marking and cutting; and explaining the importance of accuracy when designing and making, for example creating a template, measuring ingredients in a recipe, sowing seeds	Using food from the garden (p. 159) Weaving (fibre basketry) (p. 145) Make your own sundial (p. 148) Make your own hand sanitiser spray (p. 200)

Australian Curriculum: Science, Years 5 to 6

Level	Strands	Elaborations	Links
5	Living things have structural features and adaptations that help them to survive in their environment (ACSSU043)	Explaining how particular adaptations help survival such as nocturnal behaviour, silvery coloured leaves of dune plants Describing and listing adaptations of living things suited for particular Australian environments	Adaptations in garden animals (p. 95) Nocturnal animal adaptations (p. 98) Mouthpart adaptations of insects (p. 102) Adaptations in bees (p. 110) Australian native bees (p. 111) Butterflies (p. 112) Adaptations in birds (p. 114) Adaptations in common garden animal pests (p. 118) Your garden ecosystem (p. 122)
5	Scientific knowledge is used to solve problems and inform personal and community decisions (ACSHE083)	Considering how best to ensure growth of plants Considering how decisions are made to grow particular plants and crops depending on environmental conditions	Germination 1–5 (p. 28) Rate of plant growth (p. 43) Growing a bush food and bush medicinal garden (p. 135) Grow your own clothes (p. 141)
5	With guidance, pose clarifying questions and make predictions about scientific investigations (ACSIS231)	Exploring the range of questions that can be asked about a problem or phenomena and with guidance, identifying those questions that could be investigated Applying experience from similar situations in the past to predict what might happen in a new situation	Germination 1–5 (p. 28) Germination 5 (p. 37) Yeast 3 (p. 175)

continued

Level	Strands	Elaborations	Links
5	Identify, plan and apply the elements of scientific investigations to answer questions and solve problems using equipment and materials safely and identifying potential risks (ACSIS086)	Experiencing a range of ways of investigating questions, including experimental testing, internet research, field observations and exploring simulations Considering different ways to approach problem solving, including researching, using trial and error, experimental testing and creating models	Germination 1–5 (p. 28) Uses of deciduous trees (p. 61) Seasonal changes in plants (p. 62) A waste audit (p. 153) Construct a food pyramid (p. 162) Simple products to make from milk (p. 186) Minimising waste in the garden (p. 150) Classroom cookbook (p. 199) Make your own hand sanitiser spray (p. 200)
5	Decide variables to be changed and measured in fair tests, and observe measure and record data with accuracy using digital technologies as appropriate (ACSIS087)	Discussing in groups how investigations can be made as fair as possible Recording data in tables and diagrams or electronically as digital images and spreadsheets	Germination 1–5 (p. 28) Rate of plant growth (p. 43) Seasonal change in plants (p. 62)
5	Construct and use a range of representations, including tables and graphs, to represent and describe observations, patterns or relationships in data using digital technologies as appropriate (ACSIS090)	Constructing tables, graphs and other graphic organisers to show trends in data Identifying patterns in data and developing explanations that fit these patterns	Germination 3 (p. 32) Nutritional value of bush foods (p. 132)
5	Compare data with predictions and use as evidence in developing explanations (ACSIS218)	Sharing ideas as to whether observations match predictions, and discussing possible reasons for predictions being incorrect	Germination 5 (p. 37)
5	Reflect on and suggest improvements to scientific investigations (ACSIS091)	Working collaboratively to identify where methods could be improved, including where testing was not fair, and practices could be improved	Germination 5 (p. 37) Yeast 3 (p. 175)
5	Solids, liquids and gases have different observable properties and behave in different ways (ACSSU077)	Observing that gases have mass and take up space, demonstrated by using balloons or bubbles	Yeast 2 (p. 173)

continued

Level	Strands	Elaborations	Links
5	Science involves testing predictions by gathering data and using evidence to develop explanations of events and phenomena and reflects historical and cultural contributions (ACSHE081)	Developing an understanding of the behaviour of light by making observations of its effects	Germination 1 (p. 28) Make your own sundial (p. 148)
6	The growth and survival of living things are affected by physical conditions of their environment (ACSSU094)	Investigating how changing the physical conditions for plants impacts on their growth and survival such as salt water, use of fertilizers and soil types Observing the growth of fungi such as yeast and bread mould in different conditions	Germination 1–5 (p. 28) Growing mould (p. 165) What bread mould needs to grow (p. 167) Yeast 2 (p. 173)
6	Changes to materials can be reversible or irreversible (ACSSU095)	Describing what happens when materials are mixed Investigating irreversible changes such as rusting, burning and cooking	Make sourdough bread (p. 177) Make spelt bread (p. 179) Make damper bread (p. 184) Mixing materials: Water and oil (p. 74) Make gluten-free bread (p. 182) Make your own honeycomb (p. 192) Herb sauces (p. 195) Classroom cookbook (p. 199) Playdough garden decorations (p. 202)
6	Science involves testing predictions by gathering data and using evidence to develop explanations of events and phenomena and reflects historical and cultural contributions (ACSHE098)	Learning how Aboriginal and Torres Strait Islander Peoples' knowledge, such as the medicinal and nutritional properties of Australian plants, is being used as part of the evidence base for scientific advances	Bush medicine plants (p. 130) Nutritional value of bush foods (p. 132) Growing a bush food and bush medicinal garden (p. 135)
6	With guidance, pose clarifying questions and make predictions about scientific investigations (ACSIS232)	Refining questions to enable scientific investigation Asking questions to understand the scope or nature of a problem Applying experience from previous investigations to predict the outcomes of investigations in new contexts	Germination 5 (p. 37) Yeast 3 (p. 175)

continued

Level	Strands	Elaborations	Links
6	Identify, plan and apply the elements of scientific investigations to answer questions and solve problems using equipment and materials safely and identifying potential risks (ACSIS103)	Following a procedure to design an experimental or field investigation Discussing methods chosen with other students, and refining methods accordingly Considering which investigation methods are most suited to answer a particular question or solve a problem	Germination 5 (p. 37) What bread mould needs to grow (p. 167) Yeast 3 (p. 175)
6	Decide variables to be changed and measured in fair tests, and observe measure and record data with accuracy using digital technologies as appropriate (ACSIS104)	Using the idea of an independent variable (note: this terminology does not need to be used at this stage) as something that is being investigated by changing it and measuring the effect of this change Using digital technologies to make accurate measurements and to record data	Germination 5 (p. 37) Rate of plant growth (p. 43) Seasonal change in plants (p. 62) What bread mould needs to grow (p. 167)
6	Construct and use a range of representations, including tables and graphs, to represent and describe observations, patterns or relationships in data using digital technologies as appropriate (ACSIS107)	Exploring how different representations can be used to show different aspects of relationships, processes or trends Using digital technologies to construct representations, including dynamic representations	Germination 1 (p. 28) Nutritional value of bush foods (p. 132)
6	Compare data with predictions and use as evidence in developing explanations (ACSIS221)	Sharing ideas as to whether observations match predictions, and discussing possible reasons for predictions being incorrect Referring to evidence when explaining the outcomes of an investigation	Germination 1–5 (p. 28) Rate of plant growth (p. 43) Yeast 1–3 (p. 171)
6	Reflect on and suggest improvements to scientific investigations (ACSIS108)	Discussing improvements to the methods used, and how these methods would improve the quality of the data obtained	What bread mould needs to grow (p. 167) Classroom cookbook (p. 199)

Australian Curriculum: Technologies, Years 5 to 6

Level	Strands	Elaborations	Links
5–6	Examine how people in design and technologies occupations address competing considerations, including sustainability in the design of products, services, and environments for current and future use (ACTDEK019)	Evaluating the sustainability implications of materials, systems, components, tools and equipment, for example materials can be recycled or re-used to reduce waste; systems may benefit some, but disadvantage others	Minimising waste in the garden (p. 150) A waste audit (p. 153) Waste audit evaluation (p. 156)
5–6	Investigate how and why food and fibre are produced in managed environments and prepared to enable people to grow and be healthy (ACTDEK021)	Investigating and experimenting with different tools, equipment and methods of preparing soil and the effect on soil quality and sustainability including conserving and recycling nutrients, for example when designing a sustainable school vegetable garden or cropping area Experimenting with tools, equipment, combining ingredients and techniques to design and make food products or meals for selected groups for healthy eating taking into consideration environmental impacts and nutritional benefits Considering traditional and contemporary methods of food preparation used in a variety of cultures, including Aboriginal and Torres Strait Islander methods Identifying work practices that show an understanding of nutrition, environmental considerations, hygiene and food safety when designing and making a food product, for example washing fruit and vegetables carefully to remove residues, safe disposal of cooking oils to avoid environmental damage, refrigerated storage of highly perishable foods	Tools and their functions (p. 14) Tools and tasks (p. 17) Germination 1–5 (p. 28) Minimising waste in the garden (p. 150) Using food from the garden (p. 159) Construct a food pyramid (p. 162) Make sourdough bread (p. 177) Make spelt bread (p. 179) Make damper bread (p. 184) Make gluten-free bread (p. 182) Simple products to make from milk (p. 186) Herb sauces (p. 195) Classroom cookbook (p. 199)
5–6	Investigate characteristics and properties of a range of materials, systems, components, tools and equipment and evaluate the impact of their use (ACTDEK023)	Comparing tools, equipment and techniques to select those most appropriate for a given purpose	Tools and their functions (p. 14) Tools and tasks (p. 17) Germination 5 (p. 37) What bread mould needs to grow (p. 167) Make your own honeycomb (p. 192) Playdough garden decorations (p. 202)

continued

Level	Strands	Elaborations	Links
5–6	Critique needs or opportunities for designing, and investigate materials, components, tools, equipment and processes to achieve intended designed solutions (ACTDEP024)	Investigating how to minimise material use and manage waste by critiquing the environmental and social impacts of materials, components, tools and equipment	Minimising waste in the garden (p. 150) A waste audit (p. 153) Waste audit evaluation (p. 156)
5–6	Select appropriate materials, components, tools, equipment and techniques and apply safe procedures to make designed solutions (ACTDEP026)	Working safely, responsibly and cooperatively to ensure safe work areas, for example the safe use of equipment when making a water-resistant, floating craft or a model of an environmentally sensitive outdoor shelter Using appropriate personal protective equipment required for the use of some tools and equipment, for example protective eyewear Manipulating materials with appropriate tools, equipment and techniques, for example when preparing food, cultivating garden beds, constructing products	Transpiration (p. 53) Oxygen production (p. 54) Glucose production (p. 55) Starch (p. 56) Grow your own clothes (p. 141) Make your own sundial (p. 148) Yeast 1–3 (p. 171) Make sourdough bread (p. 177) Make spelt bread (p. 179) Make damper bread (p. 184)) Make your own honeycomb (p. 192) Make your own hand sanitiser spray (p. 200)
5–6	Negotiate criteria for success that include sustainability to evaluate design ideas, processes and solutions (ACTDEP027)	Evaluating the suitability of materials, tools and equipment for specific purposes	Germination 5 (p. 37) Make sourdough bread (p. 177) Make gluten-free bread (p. 182)
5–6	Develop project plans that include consideration of resources when making designed solutions individually and collaboratively (ACTDEP028)	Identifying when materials, tools and equipment are required for making the solution Reflecting on planned steps to see if improvements can be made	Germination 5 (p. 37) Make your own sundial (p. 148) What bread mould needs to grow (p. 167) Classroom cookbook (p. 199)

© Australian Curriculum, Assessment and Reporting Authority (ACARA) 2010 to present, unless otherwise indicated. This material was downloaded from the Australian Curriculum website (www.australiancurriculum.edu.au) (Website) (accessed 18 May 2021) and was not modified. The material is licensed under CC BY 4.0 (https://creativecommons.org/licenses/by/4.0). Version updates are tracked in the 'Curriculum version history' section on the 'About the Australian Curriculum' page (http://australiancurriculum.edu.au/about-the-australian-curriculum/) of the Australian Curriculum website.

PART 1
Understanding science in the garden

Creating an outside garden classroom

Gardening, along with other aspects of an outside classroom, allows teachers to instil a love for nature and for the land, and if students feel intimately involved with nature, their concern for the environment will be long-lasting. Some of the positive outcomes from building gardens are the sense of pride and accomplishment in meeting success, and feelings of self-worth as things start to grow and change occurs.

What better place is there to become partners with nature and to learn about the water cycle, nutrient cycles, native animals, natural pest control, soil and foods than a school garden? Teachers do not have to take classes long distances to observe nature. You can create gardens, bushland or mini forest areas right at the school.

Even so, there are challenges in setting up a school due to the constraints of the school system. These include resources, time, school breaks, staffing, support and the budget. Schools all have different needs, and these must be considered in the design process.

A needs analysis

A needs analysis is a process adopted by permaculture practitioners. Accessing resources and materials is an ongoing project, and this needs to be considered in the initial designing stages. In working with children and schools, you need to determine the:

- needs and wants of the children, teachers and the school

- budget (how much you can spend)

- time and energy available to implement, maintain and develop the garden area

- available resources – both onsite and in the local community

- potential site – its limitations, existing structures and positive qualities.

Teacher notes

To help you plan for building an outside classroom and how this can best be used in the school, you may like to consider and examine the following ideas:

- An energy audit of the school buildings would provide information about electricity consumption and waste in the classrooms. This could lead to the development of an energy management policy and a desire to reduce school operational costs. At all times, we are trying to teach young people about the six Rs – reduce, refuse, re-use, recycle, repair and rethink.

- As schools move deeper into environmental education, other school-directed activities follow. For example, the school may become the recycling centre for the local community where glass, paper, metals and plastic are brought in by students or their parents on a regular basis. Money raised from this venture could be invested back into the school to provide equipment and teaching resources.

- In some circumstances the school garden could become the community garden. Governments are eager for schools to make use of the currently under-utilised but extremely valuable resources that are school grounds. Parents and community members could help students with garden development or be responsible for areas themselves. They may grow things to take home or for use by the school.

One of the pleasing outcomes is that students start to teach their parents. Children soon build ponds and gardens at home, plant vegetables and develop simple earthworm farms and compost heaps after they see how easily it is done at school. The skills that children learn help build their self-esteem as they realise that they have the ability to grow things and that they have a role to play as part of a cooperative team – a role that they learn at school but that they continue to develop throughout their life as part of the local community.

Practical design considerations

The development of the school grounds should be within the parameters of the school plan or the vision for the future direction of the school. For example, if the school wants to conserve water and plant a native garden, consider native bush tucker and bush medicine plants. Many schools already have a master grounds plan. A permaculture or similar landscape design of one particular area needs to complement any existing school plans.

If a school site has natural bushland or woodland, develop a strategy to replant, maintain and protect this area. Part of your design for the school should address this issue. You may be able to develop a walk or nature trail, register the bushland as a heritage value area, or seek state or local government assistance to help preserve the area from overuse.

There are several other more practical considerations:

- **Seating is essential.** Simple log or bench seats are more than satisfactory, but rock or carved seats can look very appealing.

- **Some garden areas should be shaded.** This could be achieved through large trees, walkways, vines and pergolas. Many schools have policies about outside activities and the precautions students need to take to protect themselves from the sun, including wearing hats and sunscreen, and limiting exposure to the sun. There are great opportunities to design areas for shade so that students can safely work in the garden.

Teacher notes

- **Open, uncovered compost and manure piles could attract flies and pests.** Proper coverage of compost piles can be achieved through building a storage bay with wooden sleepers or concrete slabs that can be easily covered with hessian, carpet or underfelt. This will reduce the smell and pest problem while the compost is being made. While the end product may have a 'nice earthy smell', the process of decomposition produces a range of noxious gases if the ratio of plant and animal materials, water and oxygen is not right.

- **Water areas must be considered carefully.** Some education departments or authorities have rules and regulations, mainly for safety reasons, about water areas. Find out what these are. Your pond may have to have a weld mesh cover over it, or only a certain depth or size. Alternatively, you can build a pond but fill it with sand to make a bog garden.

- **The number of students will dictate the size of the garden.** Garden beds can vary in size, depending on how many students will tend their own plot. The typical size of a Mandala keyhole garden, for example, is not appropriate in some schools because it is a too small for a typical class. You either have to make the paths and keyholes larger or consider making a double Mandala with keyhole beds on the outside as well.

Examples of Mandala keyhole garden designs

Schools should be fun! Developing an outside classroom, where students can both learn and enjoy, is a sensible way for educators to effectively teach the curriculum. All students need stimulating lessons to hold their interest. What better way is there than to go outside and observe and learn from nature?

Background

Understanding science in the garden

Growing plants can be fun, but you do need to know what conditions they prefer so that seeds germinate and plants grow. You can conduct experiments to discover how best to grow plants in your garden. But to do that you need to understand the scientific method so you can design experiments yourself.

All experiments are based on an idea or a question that needs an answer. Examples include: Why do some seeds germinate better in the dark? Why do plants need fertiliser to grow? Such questions are often based on observations, and in many cases the answer to the question can be guessed. But is the guess the correct answer?

A scientific experiment is a way of testing an idea. The results of the experiment will either support or disprove the idea. Both types of results may lead to further studies – possibly in entirely different directions.

Evidence that disproves or does not support an idea should make scientists modify or reject their original thoughts. Support often leads scientists to extend the initial idea and to devise related experiments.

Although there are no hard and fast rules for experiments, there are components that good experiments have in common. These components are always considered when designing an experiment.

Hypothesis

When designing an experiment you must be very specific about its purpose. The question or idea to be tested should be considered as a simple statement of what is thought to be occurring. This is known as a hypothesis. Examples include: 'Aquatic plants produce more oxygen in warm water than in cold water' and 'The highest germination rate occurs when wattle seeds are soaked overnight.'

The hypothesis here could be 'Lily plants only flower in deep water.'

The hypothesis must be written so that it gives an indication of what you think is happening. You must not write it as a question. 'Does sunlight affect plant growth?' is not a hypothesis.

The hypothesis may indicate any possible relationship. So if you are trying to find out how sunlight affects plant growth, you may choose any of the following as your hypothesis:

- Sunlight causes a decrease in plant growth.
- Sunlight causes an increase in plant growth.
- Sunlight has no effect on plant growth.

Background

In each case there is a definite statement of the suspected relationship between sunlight and plant growth. The aim of an experiment is to collect data that will either support or disprove a hypothesis. For this reason, you should keep the hypothesis simple and specific. A well-stated hypothesis should indicate the type of experiment that you could carry out.

Different experiments could be set up to examine the effect of sunlight on plant growth

Usually, you write a hypothesis about one idea at a time. This is because it is much easier to design an experiment that tests only one idea. You could try to break down a complex problem into several single ideas, each with its own hypothesis.

Background

Variables

When you carry out an experiment there will be several conditions or factors that may change during that experiment. These conditions are called *variables*. You will keep some variables constant while changing others on purpose.

The *independent variable* forms the basis of the experiment and it is the factor that you change on purpose. A plant growth experiment could involve placing some plants in a dark cupboard and some in sunlight, and then measuring their growth. The independent variable would be the amount of sunlight that the plants were given. We would need to keep some factors the same, such as the size of the plants and pot, how much water we gave each plant and the temperature of the room. These variables are controlled so that they do not influence the outcome, and they are known as the *experimental variables* or the *manipulated variables*.

The *dependent variable* is the factor that changes in response to the independent variable. In the previous example, the growth of the plants depends on the amount of sunlight and is, therefore, the dependent variable. By recording the level of sunlight and measuring the growth of plants, the experimenter relates the collected data to the hypothesis.

The experiment must be designed to provide data relevant to the hypothesis. In many instances, this involves observing and measuring the dependent variable while the independent variable is deliberately changed. You can then relate any change in the results to the variable that was changed.

Background

Experimental design

Usually we set up two groups of subjects. One group has variables changed throughout the experiment and is known as the *experimental group*, and the other group has no variables changed and is known as the *control group*. The control group provides the base data with which you can make a comparison.

In the sunlight example, the control group would be the plants kept in a dark cupboard, and those left in sunlight are the experimental group.

A further example involves the hypothesis 'Aquatic plants produce more oxygen in warmer water than in cold water.' The water temperature is the independent variable, and the amount of oxygen is the dependent variable. The experimenter might place several plants in two containers. The cold temperature beaker provides the base information and is, therefore, the control. The warm beaker is the experimental set-up.

If you wanted to find out about the effect of saltwater on the growth of grass, some grass plants would be given varying amounts of saltwater solution (the independent variable), and you would measure the growth rate of the grass plants (the dependent variable). You would need to keep everything else the same for both groups, such as the temperature, volume of saltwater or water given to each grass patch, the number or size of the grass plants, the amount of sunlight given to the plants, and the volume, type and nutrition of the soil that the grass plants were placed in. All of these factors are the controlled variables.

When an experimental design does not consider a particular variable, that variable is an uncontrolled variable. In an experiment testing the effect of salt on the growth of grass, the scientist watered two different areas with either saltwater or tap water. However, he did not realise that the area watered from the tap was sometimes in the shade. The amount of sunlight is an uncontrolled variable and casts doubt on the meaning of any results. If he had made sure that both areas of grass received the same amount of sunlight, sunlight would have become a controlled variable, and the experiment would have been more effective.

Uncontrolled variables can reduce the validity of experiments, and every care should be taken to control them. The most effective way of controlling variables is to treat all groups exactly the same except for the one variable that is being tested. Another way of controlling variables is to have a large sample size, which accounts for variations in subjects. There may still be a range of results, but there is a smaller margin for error when you can identify outliers and find the mean or average.

Background

Sample size

When testing humans, factors such as age, gender, general fitness level and genetic make-up can affect results. You cannot easily control these factors just by keeping them the same. For example, an experiment that uses only 11-year-old students is controlled for age but only in a narrow sense. The results obtained from it would only relate to people who are 11 years old! To overcome these types of problems you must consider the number and composition of the subjects.

In dealing with living things you expect that there are individual differences between them. These differences may be due to genetic or environmental influences and must be taken into account when you plan an experiment. In nearly all experiments a large random sample size takes into account the variation that exists in the subjects used and increases the effectiveness of the experiment. If you chose the sample on a random basis, you would expect that the control and experimental groups would both contain a mixture of subjects. The effect of these variations would be the same for both the control and experimental groups, and any differences in the results would be due to changing the independent variable.

A large random sample should be used in experiments

As a general rule, the sample size should be as large as possible considering the cost and difficulty of conducting the experiment, and the importance of the results. For example, experiments involving new medicines have large sample sizes, while at school level the sample size is usually much smaller. An acceptable size for school experiments is usually over 10.

Once you have completed an experiment, the next important step is to repeat it to see if you or someone else obtains the same results. It is possible that some unknown factor influenced the first experiment, causing incorrect results. By repeating the experiment it is possible to check the reliability of the first set of results.

Communicating your findings

When there are major discoveries, different laboratories around the world usually repeat the original experiments. Only when all these repeated experiments come up with similar results do the discoveries become accepted. This checking and double checking is an important part of science. A good experiment produces repeatable results.

If other scientists are going to try to repeat experiments, it is necessary for the original work to be well communicated. This is usually done through scientific journals. A scientific journal is like a magazine that specialises on a single topic. It contains articles that describe the experiment and the conclusions reached. A laboratory write-up or report of one of your experiments would be similar to those published in a journal.

Safety in the garden

Clothing

Workers have to be safe in the garden. This means thinking about all the activities we do in the garden and making sure we are wearing the right clothes and using the right tools. We should wear gloves, a hat, long pants and boots. Hats and boots protect us from the harsh sun, prickly shrubs, hot surfaces and sharp edges. Other protective clothing, such as gloves and long pants, protect our skin. Other activities may require us to wear glasses to protect our eyes from objects or sunglasses to protect our eyes from the sun.

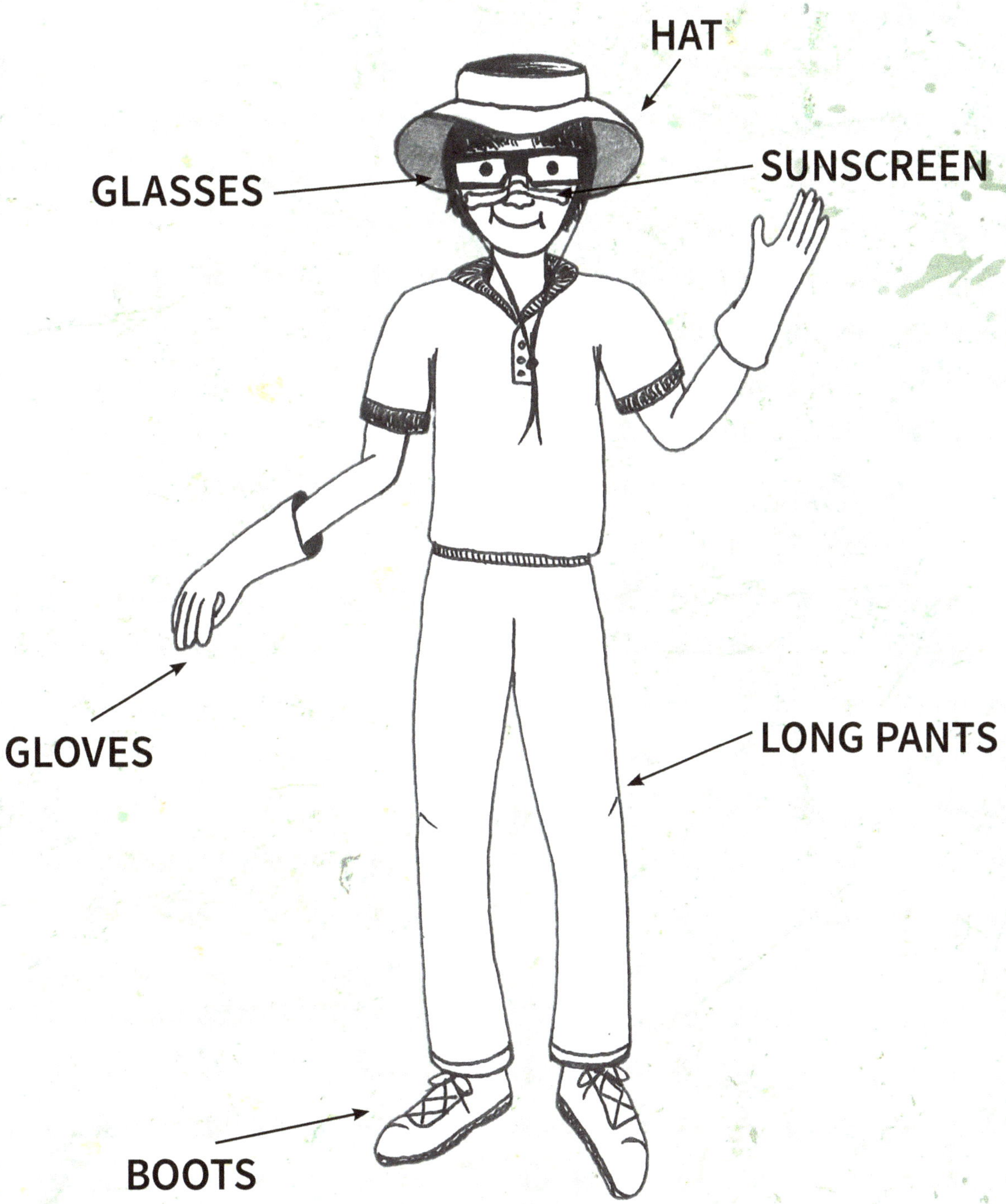

- HAT
- GLASSES
- SUNSCREEN
- GLOVES
- LONG PANTS
- BOOTS

Tools

Using tools is also another way to make sure we are safe in the garden. Tools are designed to make the job easier to avoid injuries and strain on our bodies. It is also important to make sure we are using the right tool for the job to keep ourselves and those around us safe. Many tools can be used in a garden, but the most common tools are shovels, spades, rakes, forks, watering cans, hoses, trowels and wheelbarrows.

A shovel is used to dig and move sand, compost and other soils. A shovel reduces the amount of time we spend moving these materials and can make light work of a tough job if used correctly. A trowel is similar to a shovel but is much smaller and designed to be used with one hand.

Sometimes a shovel is used to place soil in a wheelbarrow. A wheelbarrow can hold and carry many shovelfuls of soil from one place to another. This reduces the heavy lifting of moving large amounts of material around the garden and reduces the risk of injuries from repeated heavy lifting.

A wheelbarrow also allows you to mix soils and compost, which can then be placed in a garden bed. This keeps all the material in one place and avoids creating obstacles that may cause injury to others.

Rakes are a versatile tool that can be used for a number of different tasks. Rakes are most commonly used to help remove leaves, weeds and clippings from the garden but can also be used to level soil, turn soil or remove lumps. This keeps the garden safe by removing any hazards and ensuring paths are clear.

Background

Watering cans and garden hoses can be used to water plants. A hose is most effective in watering a large area. A watering can is used when watering with liquid fertiliser. After use, a garden hose should be rolled up so that workers do not trip over it, and the watering can should be put away in a safe place.

Some tools are only used in the garden. These include mulch forks, shears, loppers and weeding forks. To shift mulch, it is best to use a mulch fork, which can slide into a pile of mulch more easily than a shovel.

Shears are used for pruning in the garden. Sometimes it is necessary to cut back plants when they exceed a manageable size or during the changing of the seasons. Shears allow us to prune safely, reducing the risk of harm to both ourselves and the plant.

Loppers are another pruning tool. They have much longer handles than shears do, allowing them to reach higher places. By using loppers, we are able to reach higher areas without having to use a ladder or stretch and strain our muscles.

Weeding forks are designed to remove weeds without digging large holes in the dirt. They work by sliding into the dirt and removing the weed from the root level. They can also be useful in breaking apart clumps of soil and harvesting root vegetables such as potatoes, garlic and onions.

Tools and their functions

Examining the tools in this activity, make some observations about their size, shape and features that enable each tool to be used effectively. List the activities you would use the tool for in the garden, thinking about how the tool works and what job it might be right for. You may also examine how this tool helps make the job easier and how it can be used safely.

This activity is designed in two parts. In part 1, images of the tools are provided along with a list of the tools' names. Identify what each tool is and complete the table. In part 2, you are given a list of suggested tools and you will draw them into the table yourself. The suggested list is not a list of every single tool you might come across in the garden, meaning that the only limit in this activity is the tools you have access to.

These activities can be used in whatever way is most suitable to your class and garden.

Part 1

Hand fork   Lopper   Shears   Mulch fork   Spade   Shovel   Metal rake

	Size, shape and features	What is that tool used for?
Tool: _____		
Tool: _____		
Tool: _____		

(continued)

	Size, shape and features	What is that tool used for?
Tool: _____		
Tool: _____		
Tool: _____		
Tool: _____		

Part 2

Wheelbarrow   Watering can   Leaf rake   Hand trowel   Weeding fork

Tool	Size, shape and features	What is that tool used for?

Science in a Garden by Ross Mars I Reproducible

Tools and tasks

Based on what you have learned so far, what tools and equipment would you need for these tasks?

Task	Tools and equipment needed
Adding mulch to a garden bed	
Taking cuttings for producing more plants	
Weeding garden beds	
Planting a tree	
Making compost	

Science is observation

This project will encourage you to observe the natural world around you and record your findings and discoveries. You will also become familiar with observation as a method of gathering information and data. This project can be extended for older students with additional tools and materials or by encouraging further evaluation and problem-solving of the initial observations.

Materials

Activity sheet: Exploring your garden (p. 19)

Activity sheet: Shapes of leaves (p. 23)

Ruler or tape measure

Method

1. Explore the garden and complete the activity sheets 'Exploring your garden' on page 19 and 'Shapes of leaves' on page 23. You should observe the space around you and make your own observations and deductions to complete the activity sheets. Use measuring equipment to assess the size of leaves for the second activity sheet.

2. On returning to the classroom, discuss what you have observed and discovered with your class. Discuss any similarities or differences between student observations and why they differ. During the discussion, every student should have the opportunity to present their suggestions to the class, explaining how they came to their conclusions and why the garden would benefit from their proposed changes.

Extension

Older students may assess the garden (or surrounding areas that may be incorporated into the garden) and identify any spaces that are being under-used. Brainstorm ideas for ways that these areas could be improved to better serve the garden and school community. Alternatively, evaluate any problem areas observed during the activity, such as sections of the garden that are too shady (or too exposed to the midday sun) or areas that aren't accommodating for native wildlife. Use your problem-solving skills to find ways to improve these areas. Discuss these ideas with your class and prepare a proposal for their suggested improvements or adjustments.

Activity

Exploring your garden

Walk around your school garden or grounds and record your observations. You can also draw the various shapes of plant parts, find insects and other small animals, smell flowers and fruits, feel the soil, and discuss with your friends if you think that the garden is wildlife friendly.

Location

Our garden is found at a school that is:

☐ Inner city   ☐ Suburban   ☐ Semi-rural   ☐ Rural

Our school garden has (tick the boxes):

☐ Native bush plants   ☐ Herbs
☐ Compost area   ☐ Seating
☐ Recycling area   ☐ Flowers
☐ Food plants   ☐ Trees that provide shade
☐ Walkways and paths   ☐ Pond or bog garden
☐ Structures, such as trellises   ☐ Raised garden beds
☐ Water supply   ☐ Rainwater tank

Are there any items you think your school garden is missing?

_____
_____
_____

Site assessment

Observe the following areas and rate them on the scales provided. Circle the numbers that best match what you have observed.

Soil

Is the soil sandy, clay based or somewhere in between? Rank soil from 1 to 5.

Sand		Loam		Clay
1	2	3	4	5

What colour is the soil? Rank the colour of the soil from 1 to 5.

Dark-coloured soil				Light-coloured soil
1	2	3	4	5

Science in a Garden by Ross Mars | Reproducible

Weather

How much sun does the garden get? Is it in full sun for most of the day, or is it a mostly shaded garden? Rank the amount of sunlight from 1 to 5. This may vary for different parts of the garden, so you could circle whichever is most common or rank and label different parts of the garden.

Full sun		Partial sun		Mostly shaded
1	**2**	**3**	**4**	**5**

How much shelter and protection is available to the garden? Rank the amount of shelter and protection from 1 to 5.

Fully sheltered		Partially sheltered		Open to the weather
1	**2**	**3**	**4**	**5**

Wildlife habitat

Are there any trees in the garden that can house animals such as birds, possums and insects? Rank the number of large trees for animal habitat from 1 to 5.

Many trees and hollows		Some trees		Few trees and no hollows
1	**2**	**3**	**4**	**5**

Have the creators of this garden added any human-made animal habitats, including bee hotels, butterfly-attracting structures, frog ponds, nests or root boxes? Rank the number of human-made animal habitats from 1 to 5.

Many different habitats		Some habitats		Very few habitats
1	**2**	**3**	**4**	**5**

My observations

Describe the shape, feel, colour and smell of plants; what animals (such as insects, lizards, spiders and birds) you see; what sounds you experience; and what herbs and foods you taste. Observation involves using all your senses to gather information.

I saw _____
_____
_____
_____
_____

I smelled _____
_____
_____
_____
_____

I touched _____
_____
_____
_____
_____

I heard _____
_____
_____
_____
_____

I tasted _____
_____
_____
_____
_____

Science in a Garden by Ross Mars | Reproducible

Illustrations of the garden

Include some drawings of what you found in the garden.

Shapes of leaves

Plant leaves have many shapes and sizes. Visit the school garden and draw some of the leaves you find. You or your teacher may know some of the plant names, so include any that you know. Use a ruler to measure the leaves to compare sizes. You may also wish to add a short description of the leaf: Is it soft, spiky or rubbery? Is it thick or thin? Does it have long or short veins? These are just a few examples of the things you may notice about your leaves.

Name
_____

Name
_____

Name
_____

Name
_____

Activity

Name	Name

Name	Name

Science in a Garden by Ross Mars | Reproducible

PART 2
Growth in a garden

Seed germination (Investigations 1 to 5)

There are five different investigations students can undertake that explore factors that could affect seed germination. Four are outlined for students to give them the foundations of setting up and observing experiments. The four outlined investigations allow the comparison of:

1. light and dark
2. temperature – warm or cold
3. saltwater and tap water
4. smoke water or pyroligneous acid (wood vinegar) and tap water.

The fifth investigation allows students to develop their own hypothesis and method, make predictions and reflect on how improvements could be made. Once students have explored the scientific method in Part 1 and you have discussed experimental design, the fifth investigation ('The effect of water on germination') can be undertaken. This investigation is an open-ended task that, with your guidance, students can outline, set up and perform.

This fifth investigation encourages students to develop a method to investigate the effect of water on germination, and students may suggest several different approaches: soaking, not soaking, using different volumes of water or altering lengths of time for soaking.

About the equipment

- Petri dishes (plastic ones) are ideal but can be substituted by saucers or cut bases of yoghurt or ice cream containers.

- A roll of paper towel that can be cut up to fit dishes or tubs. You can also buy filter paper for the petri dishes.

- Aluminium foil is used to keep dishes 'in the dark'. However, a dark cupboard can be used instead of foil if the location does not alter the temperature. Be careful to monitor dishes covered in foil as these may become hotter in sunlight, which may affect results.

- You will need something to plant that can germinate quickly. Seeds that germinate within a week include mung beans and radish, while melons, squash, peas, beans take one to two weeks to germinate. The germinated peas could be used for the 'Climbing plants' activity in *Life in a garden*. Flower seeds such as zinnia, nasturtium and marigold also sprout fast. Rice, acacia and wheat are ideal for any soaking activity.

Teacher notes

Experiments with smoke water or wood vinegar

Many native plants have shown increased germination rates after soaking in smoke water. Less research has been undertaken with wood vinegar, and there is ample opportunity to conduct simple activities to investigate this substance. Both of these substances can be purchased from horticultural suppliers.

Seeds of grevillea, hakea, hibbertia, verticordia, starflowers, pimelea, dianella, leschenaultia, kangaroo/cat's paw and cone flowers have shown good responses to smoke and smoke water. Normally seeds are soaked overnight in a 10 per cent solution of smoke water, so dilute the smoke water or wood vinegar using one part smoke water or wood vinegar and nine parts water. Be aware that oversoaking or stronger solutions are not recommended as high doses of these substances may inhibit seed germination.

As many native seeds do take time to germinate, be patient, monitor the moisture of the seeds in the dishes and add water as required.

Other notes

Students may need to add a small amount of water to each dish every now and again so that the seeds don't dry out.

Once the seeds have germinated you can undertake further tests on growth rates or plant them out in the garden.

Germination 1: The effect of light on germination

Materials

Filter paper or paper towel

Petri dishes or shallow containers

Seeds (at least 20 for each group)

Tap water

Tablespoon measure (20 mL)

Aluminium foil

Method

1. Place a piece of filter paper or paper towel on the bottom of two petri dishes or shallow containers.

2. Place at least 10 seeds in each dish. Put the same number in each dish.

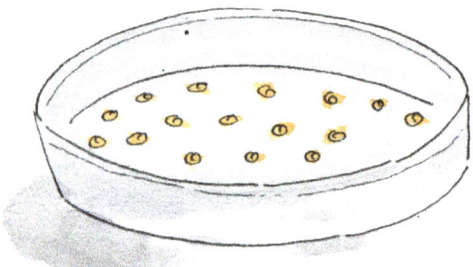

3. Add enough water to wet the paper but not flood the seeds. Usually about a tablespoon is enough (20 mL).

4. Cover one dish with aluminium foil or place in a dark cupboard. Leave the other dish exposed to some sunlight for least half a day. Ideally the dishes should be side by side or close by so that the temperature of each dish is the same.

5. Examine the seeds each day for about two to three weeks. You could expect any seeds to germinate by this time. Record the total number of seeds that sprout in each dish. Write the total number in each dish for each day that you measure. This will be a progressive (cumulative) total of all seeds that germinate, not just those that germinate on a particular day.

Results

Day	Cumulative total number of seeds that germinate	
	Light dish	Dark dish
Total		

What conclusions can you make?

_____
_____
_____
_____

Extension

Use a computer to draw a line or bar graph of your records. Use a different colour for the results of the light dish and for those of the dark dish.

Investigation

Germination 2: The effect of temperature on germination

Materials

Filter paper or paper towel

Petri dishes or shallow containers

Seeds (at least 20 for each group)

Tap water

Tablespoon measure (20 mL)

Incubator and refrigerator (or esky and ice block)

Aluminium foil

Method

1. Place a piece of filter paper or paper towel on the bottom of four petri dishes or shallow containers.

2. Place at least 10 seeds in each dish. Put the same number in each dish.

3. Add enough water to wet the paper but not flood the seeds. Usually about a tablespoon is enough (20 mL).

4. Cover two dishes with aluminium foil. Leave the other two dishes uncovered.

5. Place one covered and one uncovered dish in an incubator on low heat (20°C) or in a warm position in the classroom, such as on a windowsill. Place the other covered and uncovered dishes in a refrigerator. If there is no access to a refrigerator, place the dishes in a large esky with an ice block in it. Close the esky lid. You may need to replace the ice block each day or so.

6. Examine the seeds every few days for about two to three weeks. You could expect any seeds to germinate by this time. Record the total number of seeds that sprout in each dish. Write the total number in each dish for each day that you measure. This will be a progressive (cumulative) total of all seeds that germinate, not just those that germinate on a particular day.

Results

Day	Total number of seeds that germinate			
	Warm dish – uncovered	Warm dish – covered	Cold dish – uncovered	Cold dish – covered
Total				

What conclusions can you make?

_____

_____

Germination 3: The effect of salt on germination

Materials

Filter paper or paper towel

Petri dishes or shallow containers

Seeds (at least 20 for each group)

Tap water

Saltwater (Add 1 tbs salt to 1 cup water. Stir to dissolve. This is enough for 10 groups.)

Tablespoon measure (20 mL)

Method

1. Place a piece of filter paper or paper towel on the bottom of two petri dishes or shallow containers.

2. Place at least 10 seeds in each dish. Put the same number in each dish.

3. Add 20 mL tap water to wet the paper in one dish. Add 20 mL saltwater to the other dish.

4. Place the dishes side by side on a bench or close by so that the temperature of each dish is the same. The dishes should be exposed to some sunlight for least half of a day.

5. Examine the seeds each day for about two to three weeks. You could expect any seeds to germinate by this time. Record the total number of seeds that sprout in each dish. Write the total number in each dish for each day that you measure. This will be a progressive (cumulative) total of all seeds that germinate, not just those that germinate on a particular day.

Results

Day	Total number of seeds that germinate	
	Tap water dish	Saltwater dish
Total		

Summarise your observations.

_____
_____
_____
_____
_____
_____
_____
_____
_____
_____
_____
_____

Extension

Draw a bar graph of your results. Plot day number along the X (horizontal) axis and total number of seeds that germinate along the Y (vertical) axis. Draw bars for both tap water and saltwater, using a different colour for the lines to help distinguish them.

What conclusions can you make?

_____
_____
_____
_____

Germination 4: The effect of smoke water on germination

Fire has been part of our landscape for millennia. First Aystralians used their knowledge about plants and fire to ensure that their food sources were always available and that native grasses regenerated to provide food for animals they hunted.

While no one likes to experience severe fires and the destruction they may bring, many native plants rely on smoke or fire to germinate seed. Some species, such as eucalyptus and banksia, have hard nuts or cones that are sealed with resin. The heat of the fire melts the resin so that the seeds can eventually fall to the ground where they can germinate in a mineral-rich ash bed.

Other species of shrubs require the chemicals in the smoke to break seed dormancy. These chemicals sometimes mix with water or rain, and this triggers germination.

In this investigation you will study the effect of smoke water or wood vinegar on the germination of some native seeds. Smoke water is made when smoke from a bushfire is passed through water. Wood vinegar is a substance formed when wood is burned and the smoke, gases and liquids are collected.

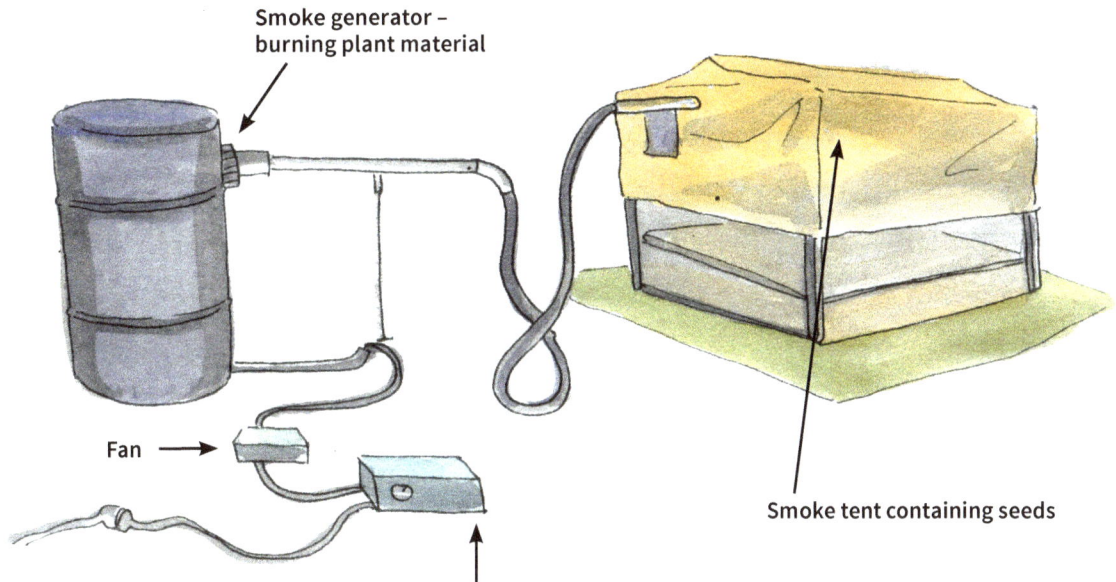

Seeds being germinated in a smoke tent

Materials

Filter paper or paper towel

Petri dishes or shallow containers

Seeds (at least 20 for each group)

Tap water

Smoke water or wood vinegar

Tablespoon measure (20 mL)

Investigation

Method

1. Place a piece of filter paper or paper towel on the bottom of two petri dishes or shallow containers.

2. Place at least 10 seeds in each dish. Put the same number in each dish.

3. Add 20 mL tap water to wet the paper in one dish. Add 20 mL smoke water to the other dish.

4. Place the dishes side by side on a bench or close by so that the temperature of each dish is the same. The dishes should be exposed to some sunlight for least half of a day.

5. Examine the seeds each week for about three to five weeks. You could expect most seeds to germinate by this time. However, the seeds of some native plants may take twice this time to germinate, so be patient. Record the total number of seeds that sprout in each dish. Write the total number in each dish at the end of each week. This will be a progressive (cumulative) total of all seeds that germinate, not just those that germinate on a particular day.

Results

Week	Total number of seeds that germinate	
	Tap water dish	Smoke water dish
1		
2		
3		
4		
5		
Total		

Summarise your findings

_____
_____
_____
_____

What conclusions can you make?

_____
_____
_____
_____

Germination 5: The effect of water on germination

Discuss with your group how you would design and perform an experiment that demonstrates the effect of water on germination. List the materials you require, your method and your predictions. Perform the experiment and discuss your findings and conclusions.

Hypothesis
_____
_____

The independent variable is: _____

The dependent variable is: _____

We need to control these variables:
_____
_____

Materials

Method

Investigation

Predictions
_____
_____
_____
_____
_____
_____

Results

Conclusions
_____
_____
_____
_____
_____
_____
_____
_____

Reflection

Discuss with your group how you could improve this activity or modify it to help you explore other ideas about factors that affect the germination of seeds. You might have some ideas about the method you used or the materials you listed, or you could suggest better ways to measure germination rates.

___

___

___

___

Digital recording

Use various digital technologies to record some of the stages and outcomes of your experiment, including taking photographs, conducting online research and recording written text. Briefly outline what you have done to incorporate digital technologies into this activity.

___

___

___

___

___

Activity

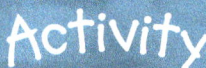

Plant parts

Observe plants in your garden and read the information provided on page 50. Label the parts of a typical plant on the drawing below.

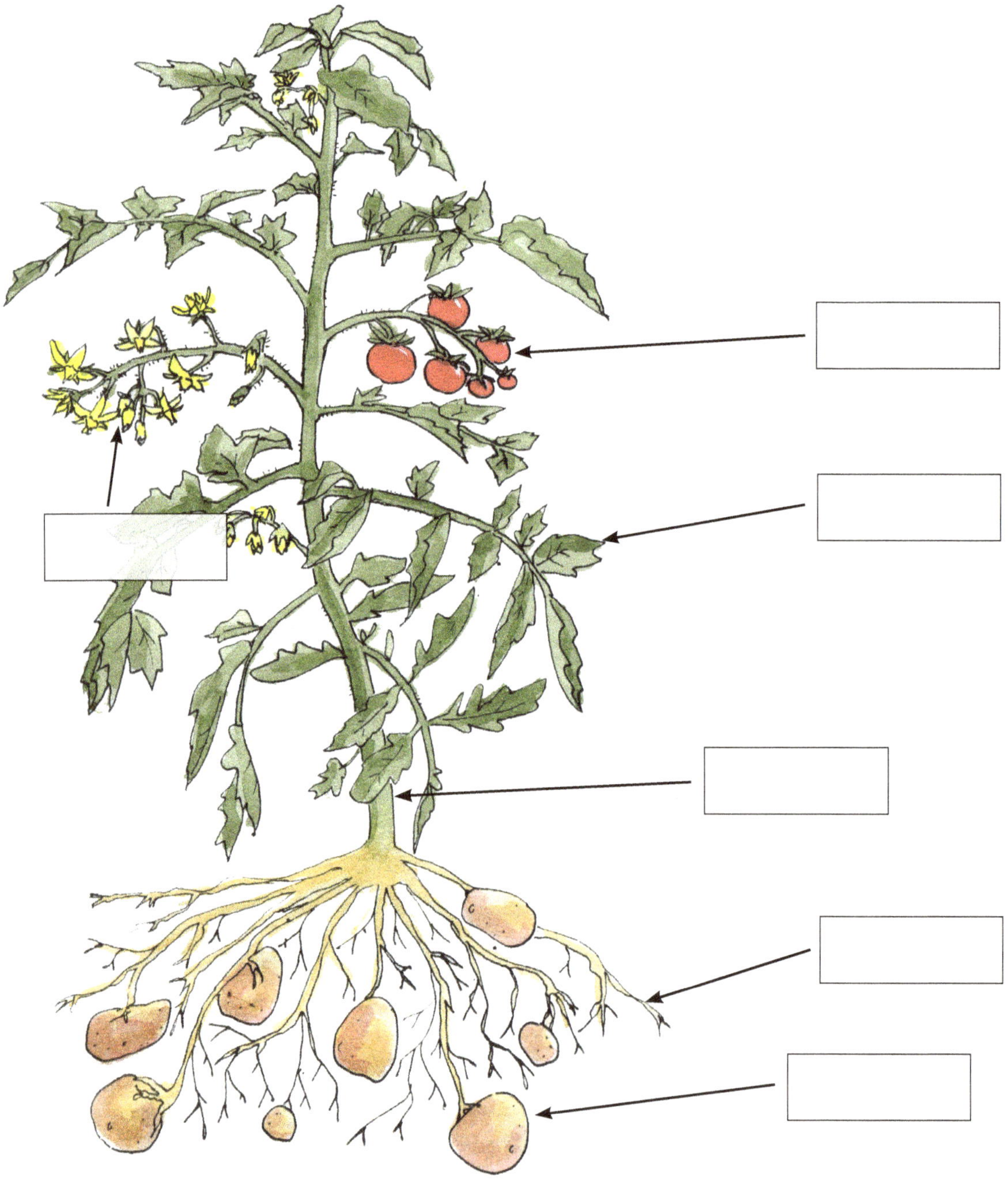

Which parts makes the fruit? ______________________________

Which part holds the plant and leaves upright? ______________________________

Which part absorbs water? ______________________________

Which part contains seeds? ______________________________

Stages of plant growth

Cut out the pictures at the bottom of this page and paste them in the correct order that shows how a seed germinates and grows into a plant. Groups may compare their orders, explain why they think each stage goes in each box and discuss their decision-making processes. If there are differing opinions across the group, work together to rework the order until the whole group thinks it is correct.

Science in a Garden by Ross Mars | Reproducible

Rate of plant growth

Students are to conduct an investigation observing the rate of growth of a plant over a month or more. They require two pots: one to serve as the control pot (with no plant) and the other to serve as the variable pot (with the plant). They will measure the amount of water given to the plant and the control pot, the height of the plant and the weight of both pots. Data should be recorded daily in the growth diary found on page 45. Students should also note their observations about the plant: the spread, number and size of the leaves; if the plant is producing any buds, flowers or fruits; and if the stem is growing in a particular direction (for example, towards the sunny side of the pot). Students may also wish to document the process with photographs or illustrations.

To further the scientific and mathematical knowledge students gain from this investigation, there are accompanying questions to answer and calculations to complete. The calculations are designed to get students to use common units and determine relationships between the multipliers – such as converting millilitres to litres and millimetres to centimetres and metres.

About the equipment

Small round or square pots (tubes) are ideal for this investigation. They should be able to fit safely in the classroom, on a windowsill or bench. The pots should also have a saucer placed underneath to avoid leaks and spills. Aluminium foil or recycled jar lids make for great and easy saucers and can be recycled after the experiment.

If this activity is undertaken in the first half of the year, choose seedlings of winter crops such as broccoli or silverbeet. If this is undertaken in second half of the year, choose summer crops such as tomatoes, capsicums or chillies. For further information on choosing crops suitable for your garden and season, you may wish to consult the planting guide in *Life in a garden* (p. 117).

Potting mix with added nutrients and a slow-release fertiliser will help support the plant growth and encourage a stronger end product to plant out in the garden.

Measuring equipment, such as measuring cylinders or kitchen scales, will also be required for students to ensure consistency in the data.

Students should use the growth diary on page 45 to record their data and observations.

If students wish to document the process with photographs, a digital camera or similar device will be needed. However, if this is not an option, students may wish to draw the changing plant in the space provided in the growth diary.

Investigation

Rate of plant growth

You will measure the growth of a plant over the course of a month or more. One pot will not have any plant but must be given the same amount of water, light and warmth as the pot with the plant. This is the control pot. You will document the water given, the height of the plant and the weight of both the plant pot and the control pot. You should also note down any observations you make about the plant and the changes as it grows. You may take photographs to digitally record the changes that occur, or you may wish to draw the plant yourself in the growth diary.

Materials

Growth diary (p. 45)

Potting mix containing added nutrients and slow-release fertiliser

50 mm tubes (small round or square pots)

Seedlings of a seasonal plant

Saucer, aluminium foil or jar lid

Measuring cylinder or jug (around 10–25 mL)

Kitchen scales

Optional: Digital camera

Method

1. Fill both pots with same amount of potting mix and weigh to make sure they are equal. Compress the soil a little with your fingers, add more potting mix and reweigh to make sure you end up with two pots weighing the same (within a few grams).

2. Add one seedling to one pot. You may have to push the soil aside or make a hole with an ice cream stick to help plant the seedling.

3. Place a saucer or dish made from the aluminium foil under each pot. This is to hold any water that may pass through.

Investigation

4. Place the pots in even sunlight, such as on a windowsill. Water the pots with the same amount of water each day (10 mL or more, as required). Adjust the measurement if you see evidence of the plant wilting, but always add the same volume of water to both pots. Record how much water you add each day.

5. Weigh both pots every few days. Wait at least four hours after watering or weigh the pots the following day. Record the weights. Measure the height of the plant and record this too. Note down any other observations.

6. The activity can be finished when the plant is about 150 mm high or has outgrown the pot.

   This should take at least a month. Weigh the pots one final time the day after the last watering.

7. Optional: Students can take progressive photographs of the plant growth over the duration of this activity. Students may choose creative ways to present this evidence at the end of the activity. If a camera is not available, students may wish to draw the plant and its changes in the growth diary.

Growth diary

Plant name:

Planted by:

Date:

Questions

The aim of this experiment is to:

_____
_____

What variables are being kept constant in the control pot?

_____
_____
_____
_____

In this activity you will be collecting data and using evidence to draw conclusions. What is the difference in the meanings of data and evidence?

_____
_____
_____

Project

GROWTH DIARY

Plant Name _____

Planted by _____

On _____

Height: _____ centimetres

Date: _____

Height: _____ centimetres

Date: _____

Front page

Project

Height: _____ centimetres

Date:

Height: _____ centimetres

Date:

Height: _____ centimetres

Date:

Height: _____ centimetres

Date:

Results

Record the changes in the pots in the table below.

Day	Volume of water added (mL)	Height of plant (mm)	Weight of pot (g)	
			Pot without plant	Pot with plant
0 (Initial weight)				

Calculations

1. If you added 10 mL water each day for the duration of the activity, what total volume of water would you have used for each pot?
   _____

2. How many litres of water have you used for both pots for the whole of the activity?
   _____

3. What is the difference in the height of the plant from the start to the end of the activity? Give your answer in millimetres.
   _____

4. How many days has the activity taken?
   _____

5. The growth rate of the plant is calculated by dividing the change in height by the number of days. What is your calculation for the growth rate? Express your answer as millimetres per day.
   _____

6. Convert the rate of growth into:

   (a) centimetres per month (30-day month)
   _____

   (b) metres per year
   _____

Conclusions

What conclusions can you make from the data you collected? What evidence is used to support these conclusions?
_____
_____
_____
_____

Recommendations

What recommendations can you make to improve this activity to make it more reliable?
_____
_____

Investigation

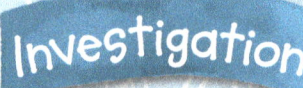

The life cycle of a flowering plant

You will document the stages of the life cycle of a flowering plant that grows in the garden. All vegetables and herbs start from a seed that germinates, grows and matures into an adult plant, and finally produces seed itself to continue the species. In this investigation you will use two different methods to observe the process and gather data.

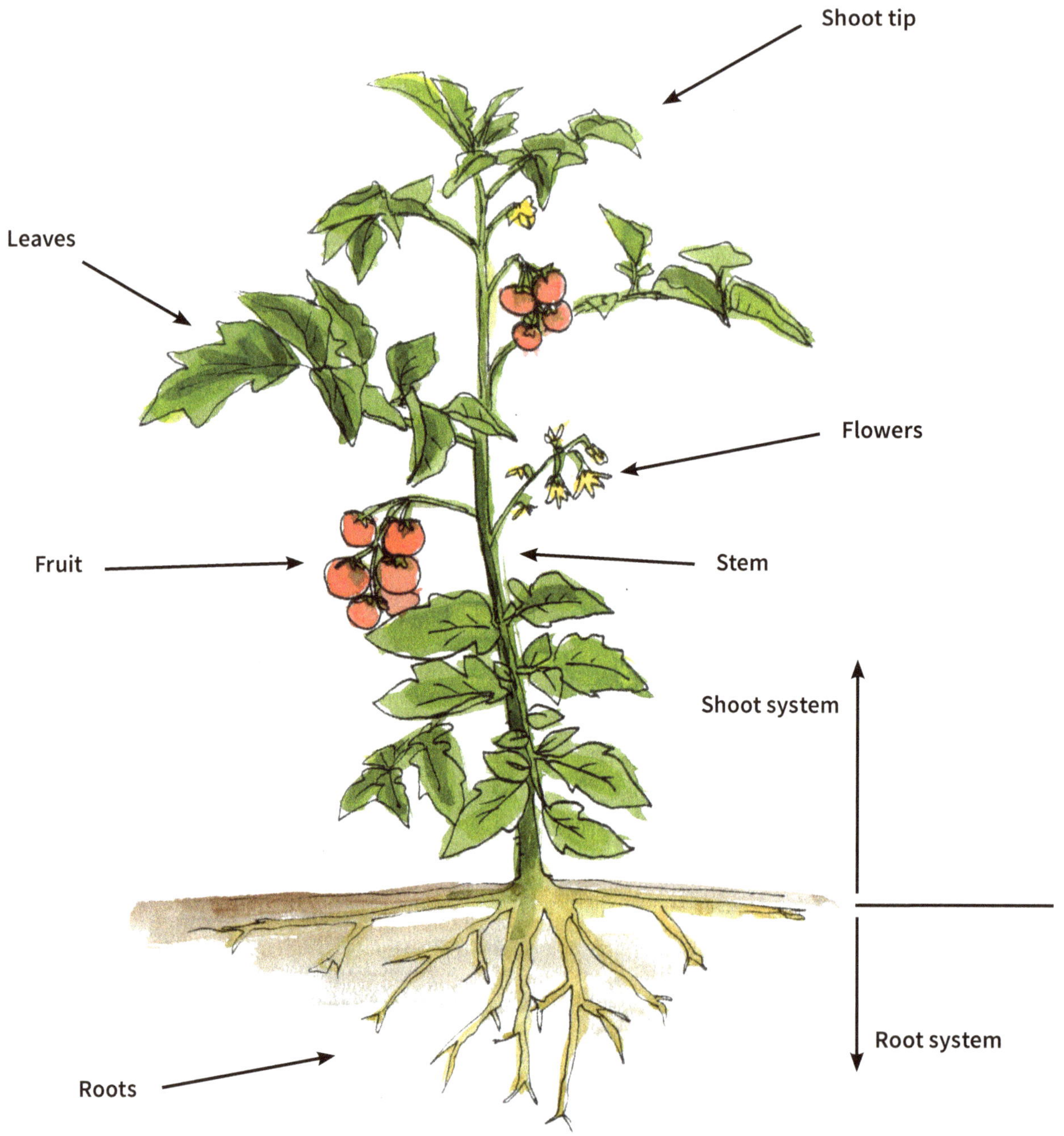

General parts of a flowering plant (tomato shown here)

Part 1

Take digital photographs during the growth of the plant. It may take several months to get enough photos of the whole process, so photograph the plant at least once a week. You may wish to print these photos and place them in sequence from seed to fruit and seed production. You could also complete this process digitally, sequencing the photos in a PowerPoint presentation or other similar style.

Extension

You may wish to re-use the photos to develop a library of the flowering plants in your garden. Once this investigation is complete, you can use the photos to create a flip book to show the life cycle of that plant.

Part 2

Set up a table (such as that shown here) in your notebook or on your computer to measure and record the height of your plant over its life cycle. Plant growth can be expressed as both height and spread (which includes the number of leaves, size of leaves, size of fruit and so on), but this investigation focuses on measuring the height over its growing season. These results will be graphed.

Your data table should have space for you to write some observations about the plant as it grows. You can use this space to record other changes related to growth, including the width of the shrub, the number of leaves each month and when fruit first forms.

Date	Height of plant (cm)	Observations

Investigation

Once your plant has matured and produced seeds, finish the investigation. Collate your photographs and your other results. Using a piece of graph paper, draw a line graph of the changes in height each week. Lay out the scale and axis as shown here.

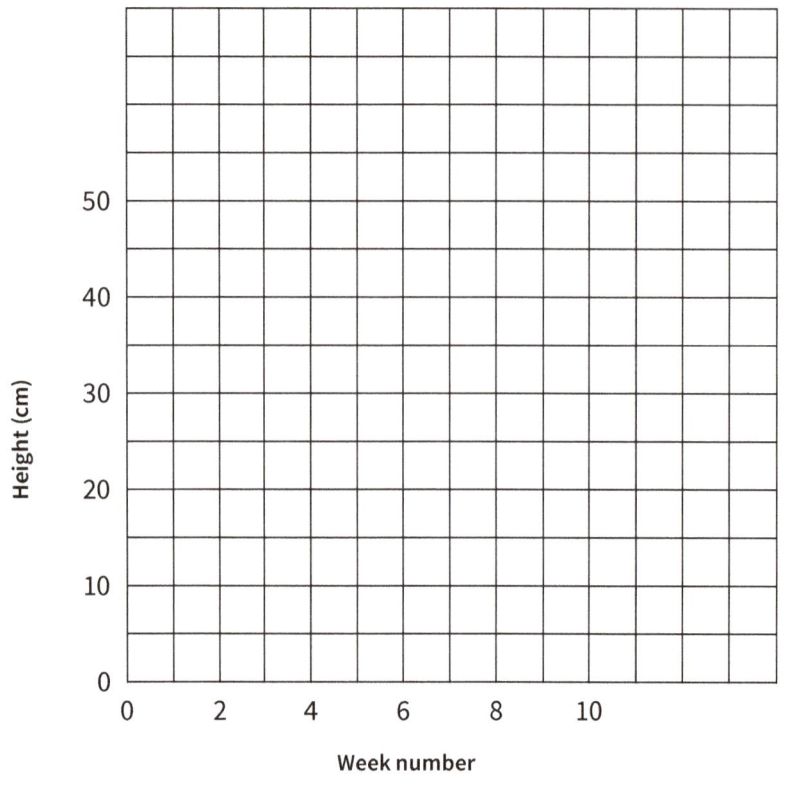

TIP: Make sure you label each axis evenly, using at least two-thirds to three-quarters of each axis for the scale you choose.

Results

Summarise your observations and results.

_____
_____
_____
_____

If we wanted to accurately measure the growth of a plant over time, what would we need to do? What might we need to consider when thinking about growth?

_____
_____
_____
_____

Investigation

Transpiration

Transpiration is the plant process that moves water through a plant and eventually out through the leaves, stems and flowers. Transpiration helps to cool plants down and helps nutrients move around inside a plant, from the roots to the shoots. In this investigation students will study transpiration by collecting the transpired water.

Materials

Large plastic bags

Cable ties or nursery tie wire

Plants to test (with large leaves if possible)

Method

1. Slip a large plastic bag over some leaves on a small branch. Use tie wire or another tie to wrap the neck of the bag to the branch. Tie the wire tight but do not damage the bark.

2. Leave this set-up for at least one day. Inspect it to see if water accumulates in the bag. You can keep the bag over the leaves for several days with no damage to the plant.

Extension

There are many different factors that may impact a plant's transpiration. These include the number of leaves a plant has, the size of the leaves, the number of stomata on each leaf (the pores through which leaves lose water), the sunlight the plant receives, the temperature and humidity of the environment, and the plant's access to water. You may want to discuss how each of these variables could increase or decrease transpiration. You may also wish to test this investigation across a range of plants and compare observations and results.

Investigation

Oxygen production

Plants use sunlight, water and carbon dioxide (in the air around us) to create their own food. During this process, the plant also makes oxygen. Oxygen is then released through the leaves and into the air. This process is called *photosynthesis*, and oxygen is a by-product of the process. Since all humans and animals need oxygen to breathe, this is a very important process. In this investigation, students will observe oxygen bubbles on the leaf of an aquatic plant. It is not necessary to test and confirm that this is oxygen.

Materials

Large beaker or wide-mouthed jar

1 soft leaf (freshly picked of a submergent – aquatic – plant, such as species of genus *Vallisneria* and genus *Pogostemon*, but floating aquatic plants are also an option)

Pencil or glass rod

Optional: Small stone

Optional: Hand lens or magnifying glass

Method

1. Half fill a jar with water. Pick a leaf and place it upside down in the jar (the bottom of the leaf should be facing upwards). Push the leaf with the pencil or glass rod under the water surface. You may have to use a small stone to keep the leaf under the surface.

2. Leave the jar in a sunny place for the day. Periodically look for any evidence of bubbles on the leaf surface. You might need a hand lens or magnifying glass to see it. Use the glass rod or pencil to gently tap the leaf and you might see bubbles become dislodged.

Extension

There are many different factors that can determine when and how much oxygen a plant produces. These can include the size of the leaves, whether stomata are on one side of both sides of the leaves, and how much heat, energy and sunlight the leaves are exposed to.

These factors are explored in the following extension tasks:

- Try this experiment with different types of leaves of varying shapes and sizes.
- Place some leaves both upside down and the right way up. Observe if bubbles can still be seen.
- Use hot water (warm to touch) for the experiment instead and see if any bubbles appear.
- Place some leaf jars in the dark instead of in a sunny position.

Investigation

Glucose production

The photosynthesis process described in the previous investigation produces food for the plant in addition to oxygen for other living things. This food is glucose, which is a simple sugar. These sugars are produced and can be found in the leaf. In this investigation students will test for sugars in leaves. The experiment is straightforward but it does require some chemicals and equipment.

Materials

Freshly picked leaf

Scissors or Stanley knife

Mortar and pestle

Test tube

Benedict's solution, Fehling's solution or Tollens' reagent

> Note: All of these can be sourced online, through scientific or chemical supply stores, or from the local secondary school. All three require heating as part of the test for glucose.

Test tube tongs or holder (wooden or steel)

Source of heat (methylated spirits burner, Bunsen burner, other camp gas burner)

Method

1. To test glucose in a leaf you need to choose a freshly picked leaf. Cut the leaf up as much as possible, mash with a mortar and pestle and place the contents in a test tube.

2. Add enough Benedict's solution (or Fehling's or Tollens') to cover the leaf. Using your heat source safely, gently heat the test tube until boiling, then continue to heat for another minute or two. If glucose is present, the blue solution changes colour to orange or red-brown. (A precipitate forms with the colour depending on how much and type of sugar present.)

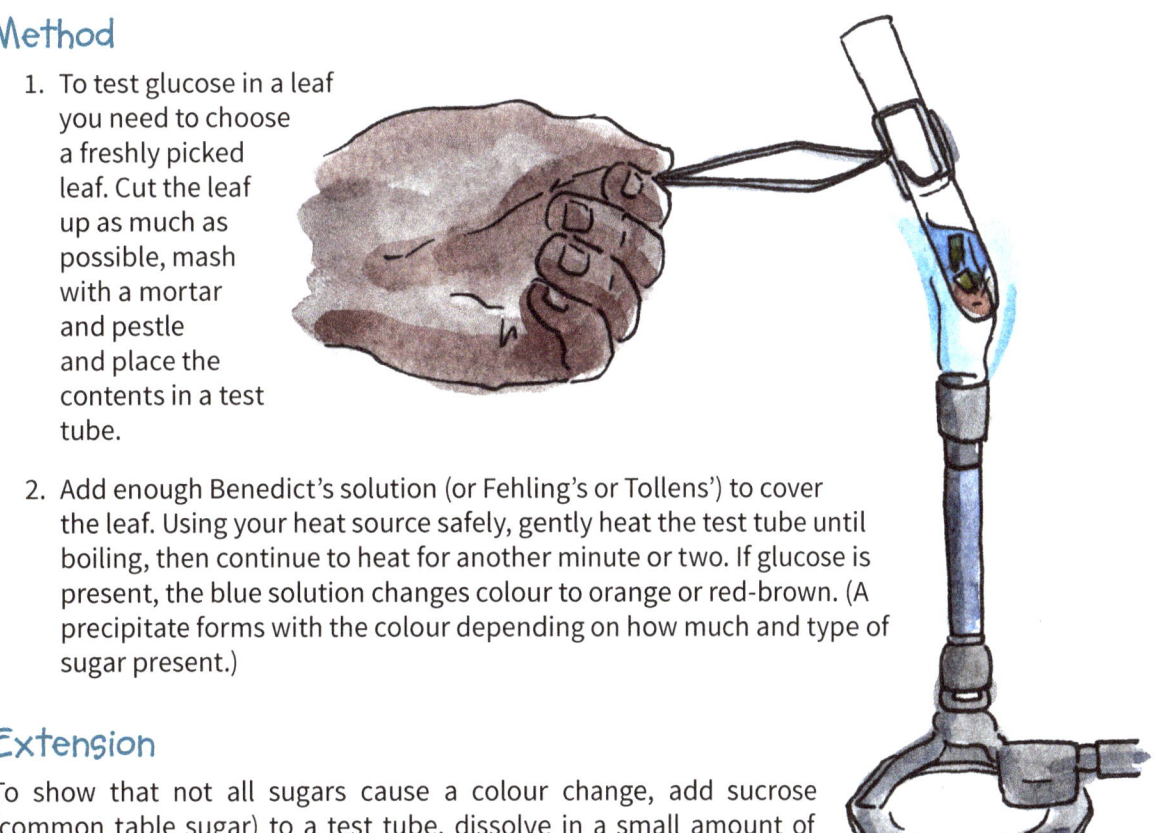

Extension

To show that not all sugars cause a colour change, add sucrose (common table sugar) to a test tube, dissolve in a small amount of water, add Benedict's and repeat the procedure. The blue colour should not change.

Starch

When leaves manufacture glucose, excess glucose is converted into starch, which can be stored in the leaf and used when required. In this investigation you will test for the presence of starch in a leaf.

Materials

Freshly picked leaf

Hot water

Kitchen tongs (or tweezers)

Jars or glass petri dish (and lid)

Methylated spirits or acetone

Cling wrap

Old household plates to hold solution on top of a leaf (You could make your own shallow aluminium foil dish.)

Iodine solution (sourced from chemical suppliers)

Method

1. Pick a fresh leaf and blanch it in hot (near boiling) water for 10 seconds. (This stops all cell reactions. Cell reactions continue after a leaf has been picked from the plant, and it is important to stop these reactions to complete the experiment.)

2. Use tongs to remove the leaf safely, then place it into a jar with methylated spirits or acetone (enough to cover the leaf). Cover the jar with cling wrap or a lid to prevent solvent from evaporating away.

3. After all pigments and colour are removed (or nearly so), use tongs or tweezers to place the leaf onto a plate, cover with iodine solution and leave for 10 minutes.

4. Lift up the leaf (with the tongs to avoid staining your hands), wash to remove stain and then examine the leaf for dark patches. Starch is turned blue-black by iodine. Record your observations. You may even take photos of your results.

Extension

It is possible to convert starch back into glucose. There are a couple of ways to do this, but the simplest is to chew a cracker biscuit for as long as you can without swallowing anything (at least a few minutes). You should then spit everything into a petri dish and leave for 15 to 30 minutes.

While you are waiting, take another cracker, break it up and place half of the pieces into one of two test tubes. Use the Benedict's and iodine solutions (separately) to test for glucose and starch in the biscuit.

Split the chewed cracker biscuit into two test tubes and perform the glucose and starch tests. There may be less starch and hopefully more glucose in the results.

PART 3

Changes in the garden

Background

Seasons

In Western cultures, there are four seasons in one year: summer, autumn, winter and spring. In some countries *autumn* is also called *fall* as this is when some plants lose their leaves, and this is when they 'fall' from the tree. These seasons divide the year into four equal parts.

Since Australia is very diverse in its climate, these seasons may not always accurately align with the weather patterns of local areas. In many First Australians cultures there are a variety of different seasons depending on the geographical and ecological region in question. Seasons are based on changes in weather patterns as well as changes in the environment, landscape and wildlife across the year. As these seasons are linked to the natural events that occur in that region, for some cultures there can be six or seven seasons, while other regions that experience less change across the year may have as few as three. The names of seasons are also reflective of the dialect of the people, the events occurring (such as cold weather or rain) or resources available during that season (such as when particular plants flower or fruit).

Understanding the seasons and how to work in harmony with the environment is an important part of managing and maintaining our gardens and bushlands, and ensuring we are engaging with the environment in sustainable ways.

The seasonal calendar for First Australians

Identify the traditional owners of the land where you live. Undertake a research project to discover the seasons of that group and how this influences the way people interact with the environment. You may also wish to invite an Elder (someone who is recognised as a custodian of knowledge and beliefs) to your school to discuss the local area and the cultures in that region.

The seasonal calendar includes the Western months and seasons and allows space for you to complete the table with the seasons of the First Australians culture of your area and note any observations you make or facts you learn about those seasons.

	Western terms	**First Australians cultures**
Month	Season	
December	Summer	
January		
February		
March	Autumn	
April		
May		
June	Winter	
July		
August		
September	Spring	
October		
November		

1. During which season of the completed First Australians calendar does your birthday fall?
   _____

2. What is the wettest season in your area? List both Western and First Australians terms.
   _____

Extension

Extend the table of seasons to include other First Australians cultures from elsewhere in Australia, focusing on a diverse range of regions and environments. Compare their seasons as well as their climate and landscape. You may note observations on the similarities and differences you identify. How do these different seasons and weather patterns change how the cultural groups interact with, and care for, the land?

Background

Changes in the garden

Plants change with the seasons. As the day and night temperatures fall, many plants respond by losing their leaves. They store food in their stems, branches and roots to help them survive the cold winter months. When the daytime temperatures start to rise again, new growth occurs, and the plants make new leaves and grow taller.

Instead of losing their leaves, some plants instead go dormant during less ideal growing conditions to conserve resources. When a plant starts to become dormant, some leaves change colour. As the leaves change, stored substances are also absorbed back into other parts of the plant.

Other trees keep their leaves all year round and are called *evergreen trees*. Evergreen trees provide shade all year round. Most Australian shrubs and trees are evergreen.

Many common vegetables and herbs only live for one year, and as the seasons change they go through their life cycle and eventually die. As part of their life cycle, plants produce seeds so that new plants can grow.

The level of change in the environment depends on where you live. Those living in the tropics of northern Australia tend to have similar weather across the year, while those living in the southern parts of Australia have the greatest seasonal change. Areas closer to the equator have fairly constant sunlight in each season, but regions both north and south of the equator experience hotter summers and cooler winters. Due to the tilt of Earth's axis, the two hemispheres experience the seasons at different times of year; for example, as the Northern Hemisphere experiences summer, the Southern Hemisphere has winter.

The other changes that occur in the garden can be due to insect and animal activity. The life cycle of many plants is closely linked to that of particular animals that may be pollinators or seed dispersers. Many insects breed and become active in warmer months, so spring is when many flowering plants are pollinated. However, other plants flower in summer, winter or autumn depending on their environment.

Gum trees are evergreen – they have leaves all year round

Plants pass through their life cycle as they respond to the length of daylight. They have chemicals in the growing tips (the top of the stem and leaf shoots where all growth starts) that detect the presence and level of light. Some flowering plants also sense the length of night as a signal to flower. It is these changes in light intensity that trigger the seasonal changes in plants.

Many plants, such as this chestnut, produce flowers then fruits (or nuts) as the seasons change

Uses of deciduous trees

Deciduous trees typically lose their leaves in late autumn and early winter as an adaptation to extreme cold. This is because frost and extreme cold may kill the leaves of the plant. There are a few trees in northern Australia that lose their leaves in summer as an adaptation to extreme heat, including white cedar and the boab tree. Some deciduous trees provide fruit, others showy flowers. Some are used as shade trees or for furniture and timber.

This task is a research assignment where you choose one of the listed trees and find out about its characteristics: ultimate height and spread, preferred growing conditions (soil type and climate), and products and uses.

Your teacher may allocate a particular plant to you so that the class covers all listed trees. Their scientific names are given as well. Scientific names often give clues about a plant's characteristics. For example *nigra* means *black*, so this is used for black mulberry and black walnut as well as describing the black berries of the elderberry. *Domestica* means *domesticated* or *tamed*, so ancient types of apples and plums have now become the common fruits we eat today. People use common names to differentiate particular varieties, so when you say 'apple' (all of which are *Malus domestica*), which variety of the many hundreds (such as Granny Smith, Red Delicious and pink lady) are you referring to?

- Japanese maple (*Acer palmatum*)
- Honey locust (*Gleditsia triacanthos*)
- Japanese raisin tree (*Hovenia dulcis*)
- Prune (*Prunus domestica*)
- Sugar maple (*Acer saccharum*)
- Elderberry (*Sambucus nigra*)
- Black mulberry (*Morus nigra*)
- Maidenhair tree (*Ginkgo biloba*)
- Box elder (*Acer negundo*)
- Black walnut (*Juglans nigra*)
- Fig (*Ficus carica*)
- Liquidambar (*Liquidambar styraciflua*)
- White poplar (*Populus alba*)
- English oak (*Quercus robur*)
- Wisteria (*Wisteria sinensis*)
- Chinese tallow (*Triadica sebifera*)
- Cherry tree (*Prunus avium*)
- Apple (*Malus domestica*)
- Powton (*Paulownia fortunei*)
- Chestnut (*Castanea sativa*)
- Walnut (*Juglans regia*)
- Pistachio (*Pistacia vera*)
- Curry leaf (*Murraya koenigii*)
- Pomegranate (*Punica granatum*)
- Quince (*Cydonia oblonga*)
- Indian bean (*Catalpa bignonioides*)
- Desert ash (*Fraxinus oxycarpa*)
- Neem (*Azadirachta indica*)
- Weeping willow (*Salix babylonica*)
- Chinese elm (*Ulmus chinensis*)
- Drumstick tree (*Moringa oleifera*)
- Claret ash (*Fraxinus angustifolia*)

Japanese maple

Pomegranate

Liquidambar

Seasonal changes in plants

This activity is undertaken over several seasons. You are to photograph a particular tree that you know is deciduous so that you can record the changes that occur in the plant as seasons change. This may include changes to leaf colour; the number of leaves on the tree; flowering, fruiting and seed production; and new growth (shoots). Examples of trees that have remarkable colour changes include Chinese toon (*Toona sinensis*), liquidambar (*Liquidambar styraciflua*), Japanese maple (*Acer palmatum var. atropurpureum*), sugar maple (*Acer saccharum*) and red maple (*Acer rubrum*).

Select approximately 10 photographs that best represent the events and changes that occurred from the beginning of the year to the end. Print and mount these as a timeline.

Changes in Chinese toon – Toona sinensis

Background

Water in the garden

All living things need water.

Water supports all life. Animals and birds drink water so that their bodies can work well. Fish and frogs swim in water. Some animals cannot survive out of water.

Rain falls from clouds and wets the ground. Rain on the ground enters the soil. Some water might not enter the soil but flow across the surface. Water that enters the soil slowly flows underground.

Water transports minerals from the soil. Minerals are used to make plants grow and produce substances that plants use.

Some plants can store water in their stems, such as cacti. Other plants may store water in their leaves or roots. Plants use this water to make food.

Sometimes there is not enough water to make things grow. Plants may stop growing and even die if they do not have access to water in the soil.

Many foods we eat contain water. Eggs, lettuces and melons contain lots of water, while bananas, apples and apricots contain less.

Without water there is no life.

Teacher notes

About water

Teachers should introduce the topic with a discussion about the importance of water. Students can read the background information 'Water in the garden' (p. 63), which provides a good overview of the topic.

Students may then be able to tackle the worksheet 'What is so important about water?' (p. 65), where they can think about where water is used, where it comes from, why every living thing needs it and how much is found on Earth.

The activities about water will also help explore the concepts of measurement and time.

What is so important about water?

Life does not exist without water. Have a think about how important water is and answer these questions.

Where do you get water from every day?

_____
_____
_____
_____
_____

List three ways we use water every day.

_____
_____
_____

Why is water important to plants and our gardens?

_____
_____
_____
_____
_____

How much water covers the Earth? Colour in or shade three of these four segments. This is how much water covers the Earth's surface.

What fraction is this?

_____

Science in a Garden by Ross Mars | Reproducible

Water cycle processes

The water cycle is the way water moves around our Earth. Since the world has limited sources of water, the water cycle is the ultimate method of water recycling. Water moves between rivers, oceans, other bodies of water, the land and the atmosphere in a constant cycle. As it goes through this cycle, it goes through many different forms. It can be a liquid (in the form of water and rain), a gas (in the form of vapour) or a solid (in the form of ice and hail).

The water cycle has many terms that describe the various processes of how water enters and leaves the atmosphere. Evaporation, condensation, cloud formation, precipitation, collection and combustion are all part of the water cycle.

The sun is the main source of energy that drives the water cycle. Energy from the sun heats up bodies of water and increases their temperature. When this happens, some of the water turns into vapour and is released into the atmosphere. This process is called *evaporation*. Plants also lose some water through the process of transpiration, which was explored earlier.

When this water vapour is released into the atmosphere it rises into the sky. As it gets higher, it cools and returns to its liquid form. This process is called *condensation*. This liquid joins together and becomes clouds in a process called *cloud formation*.

As more water joins the clouds, it becomes too heavy for the air to hold all the liquid. The liquid then falls as rain. If it is very windy and cold, some water droplets may freeze and fall as hail. The cold may also allow ice crystals to form and fall as snow. Falling rain, hail and snow is known as *precipitation*.

Water falls in many different places. It can fall back into bodies of water, where it begins the evaporation process again, fall somewhere cold and become part of a glacier, fall onto plants and trees, helping the root systems grow, or soak into the soil. Water that is found in the soil is called *groundwater*.

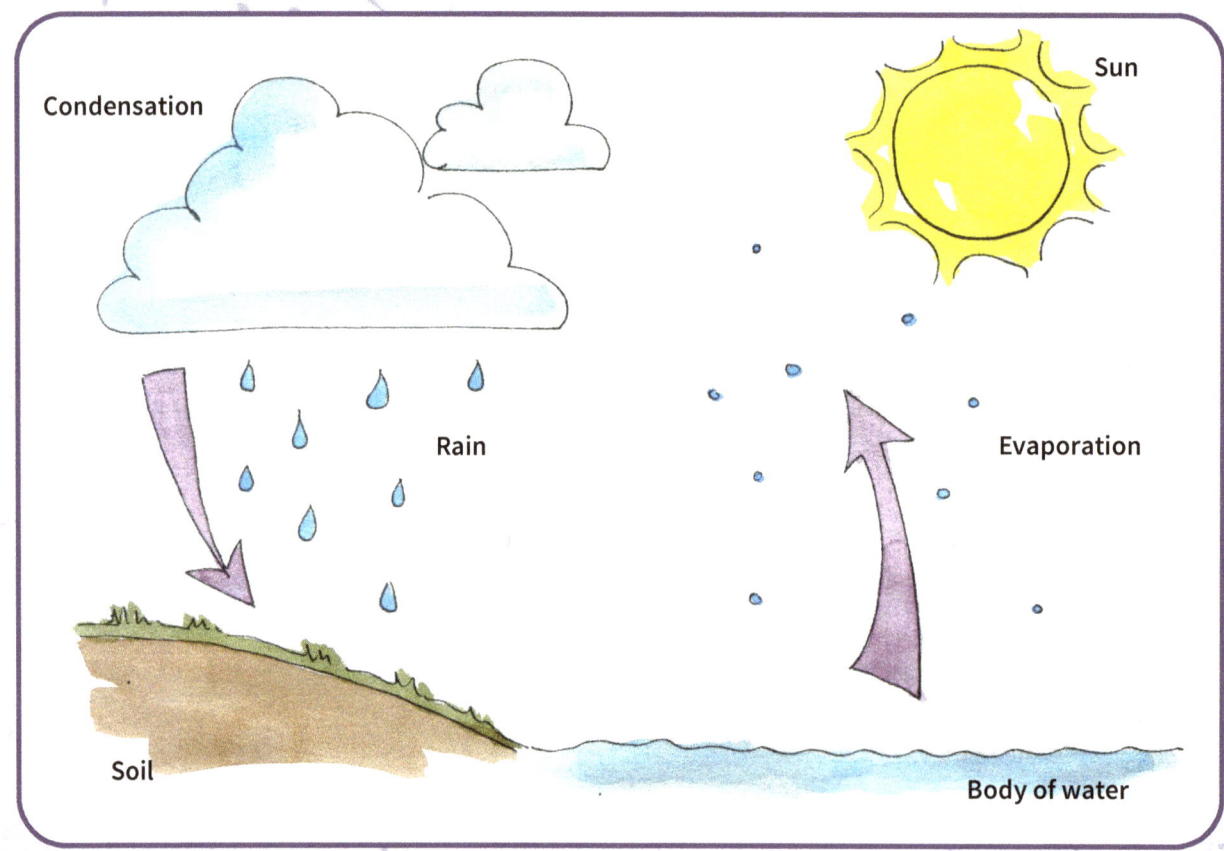

The water cycle process

Investigation

The water cycle (in a bag)

In this investigation you will explore the water processes discussed on page 66. This investigation is designed to be completed in groups.

Materials

1 plastic resealable sandwich bag

¼ cup water

Measuring cup or jug

Blue food colouring

Tape

Optional: Markers

Method

1. Source a snap lock or resealable bag that will be able to hold water without leaks. Decorate the bag with a sun and cloud if you wish to highlight the processes that occur in the bag and have a visual reminder of the elements of the investigation.

2. Add ¼ cup of water to the bag. Add four drops of food colouring to the water, avoiding any spills as the food colouring may stain.

3. Ensure the bag is tightly closed with no leaks or air flow but allow some air to stay in the bag. Shake the bag around to spread the liquid and leave droplets inside the bag.

4. Tape the bag to a window in the classroom that gets plenty of sun. You should now be able to observe the water go through the water cycle in the bag. Document the changes you see occurring in the bag. Discuss with your classmates what you see happening.

Extension

You should notice the water droplets on the side of the bag are not blue but clear during the water cycle process. Can you explain why?

The water cycle (in a cup)

This is another investigation that explores the water cycle, but this one allows the process to occur more quickly and be more closely observed. This investigation may be more suited to older students.

Materials

250 mL beaker or clear glass cup (it needs to be able to hold boiling water)

Large kettle or urn

Water

Saucer or watch glass

Ice cubes

Torch

Method

1. Prepare the boiling water by filling and turning on the urn or kettle. Pour the boiling water into the glass.

2. As soon as the hot water is in the glass, cover the opening immediately with the watch glass or saucer and place two or three ice cubes on top. The set-up should look like this:

3. Look into the glass and make observations. You can use a torch to show more detail of what is happening. You should notice condensation under the saucer, possibly some vapour (representing clouds) and some drops falling back into the glass or down the sides of the glass (precipitation). Occasionally you might see a convection current as water evaporates from the water surface, rises, condenses and falls back.

Summarise your observations here: _____
_____
_____
_____
_____

What is the role of the ice cubes on top of the saucer?
_____
_____
_____

Why do we need a torch?
_____
_____
_____

Extension

Water is both 'cleaned' and 'contaminated' during various stages of the water cycle. Pure water first evaporates and condenses in the atmosphere. Sometimes dust and chemicals combine with water in the clouds, and rain maybe a little acidic or have a dust particle nucleus. As water moves through the soil it is filtered. Water containing fine clay particles (murky brown water) can be stripped of soil and emerge much cleaner.

You can explore water purification through an activity where murky water (made from small amount of clay shaken in a jar of water) is poured through some garden soil, potting mix or even plain sand. Place the soil in a filter paper and funnel, pour the murky water slowly into it and capture the purer water that comes out.

Investigation

How does water get clean?

How does water get clean? When water falls to the ground it can become a muddy puddle. And when it falls in a river, that river can be full of sticks, leaves and other things. So why isn't rain dirty? This investigation will explore why.

Materials

Dirt or garden soil

Warm water

Mixing bowl

Plastic (stretch) wrap

Clear drinking glass (must be shorter than your mixing bowl)

Small marble or pebble

Optional: Measuring cylinder (for measuring volume)

Method

1. Fill the mixing bowl to about two-thirds full with dirt.

2. Add the warm water to the dirt, pouring evenly to make a moist mixture throughout. The mixture should be thoroughly wet but still strong enough to hold up a glass.

3. Place the empty glass face up carefully in the middle of the mixture. The top of the glass should be a couple of centimetres below the mixing bowl lip.

4. Cover the bowl in plastic wrap, making sure to seal the edges tightly to avoid losing any vapour.

5. Place the bowl in a sunny or warm position. Direct sunlight works best, as the heat energy from the sun is what encourages evaporation.

6. Place the marble or pebble in the centre of the plastic wrap above the cup. This will help the direct the water condensation into the cup for collection. Make sure the marble or pebble doesn't let the plastic wrap dip too low and seal off the cup.

7. Check the experiment regularly. The cup should start to collect water anywhere between 30 minutes to an hour after you have finished setting it up. You may wish to leave for a full day to assess how much water you collect.

Observations

What does the collected water look like?

_____
_____

How long did you leave the investigation for?

_____

How much water did you collect (in millilitres)? If you have recorded the time you started to the time you finished, you can calculate how much water is collected each hour.

_____
_____

Based on your calculation of water collected per hour, how much water could you expect to collect over 24 hours?

_____
_____

Discuss as a class how you think the experiment works. Record some of the answers here.

_____
_____

Even though it has been cleaned, this water should not be drunk by students. Why might this be?

_____
_____

How does it work?

Water is made of very small parts that can only be seen when they are grouped together as a droplet. When water evaporates during the water cycle, the water separates into its very small parts again – the vapour. The vapour gets carried into the atmosphere, but dirt, sticks and leaves are all too large to be carried with it. This means that the vapour and other objects are separated and the water vapour is purified, giving us fresh clean water.

Extension

1. Research *solar stills*. Investigate the design and function of a solar still, typically used to get fresh water from sea water.
2. Find out how you can obtain water in the wild using plant leaves.

Movement of rain

This is a simulation to show how rain falls from clouds. Shaving foam represents clouds and food colouring drops represent rain as it falls down. Rain falls when clouds cannot support the weight of water droplets, and they fall to the ground. Rain is not shaped like tear drops as many believe. Gravity, surface tension and air pressure cause the rain drops to be flattened at the bottom and more rounded at the top.

Materials

Jar and lid (500 mL)

Water

Foam shaving cream

Food colouring

Method

1. Fill a jar to three-quarters with water. The jar should be positioned on a bench so everyone can see from the side.

2. Spray shaving cream across the top in a layer about 1 to 2 cm thick (not above the jar rim). If you only have shaving gel, rub a small amount between your hands to lather this up as a foam and scrape it into the jar. Wash your hands before proceeding.

3. Add a few drops of food colouring to different areas of the foam. Observe. The food colouring will pass through the foam and sink downwards.

4. Discuss what you are observing as a class.

Investigation

Cyclone in a jar

Cyclone is the term for very low-pressure systems in the Southern Hemisphere that typically rotate clockwise. In the Northern Hemisphere, these systems turn anticlockwise and are called *tornadoes*. However, rarely, some turn in the opposite direction in each hemisphere. These anticyclones have a high-pressure centre. Cyclones are also known as *hurricanes* and are typically formed in tropical regions.

Materials

Jar and lid (500 mL)

Dishwashing liquid

Water

Vinegar

Glitter

Teaspoon

Method

1. Fill a jar to three-quarters with water.
2. Add one teaspoon of dishwashing liquid.
3. Add one teaspoon of vinegar.
4. Sprinkle a pinch of glitter into the jar.
5. Screw on the lid. Shake the jar in a swirling motion for a few seconds and then hold to observe the spiral that occurs.
6. Try swirling clockwise first and then anticlockwise at another time to see if any differences can be noted. (In both cases a vortex is seen.)

A vortex forms as a result of various forces (such as gravitational or centrifugal forces) and the velocity of the moving water, making water move in one direction and increasing in speed towards the taper.

The glitter has a few useful purposes. It enables you to better see the water swirling around. As the water slows the glitter particles will fall to the bottom of the jar, but you will notice that they tend to collect in the middle of the jar – at the base of a vortex.

Mixing materials: Water and oil

There are three basic types of liquids: those that mix with water, those that mix with oil (and don't mix with water) and those that mix with both water and oil. Detergents work by mixing with both water and oil (or grease), and that is how dishes can be cleaned in the kitchen sink.

Water is denser than oil, so if you put water and oil in the same container, the water will sink to the bottom. You could try this activity with food colouring powders and oil-based solutions, and the observations will be different again.

Materials

Baby oil or other mineral oil

> Note: Both oils are colourless. Food-grade mineral oil is used to wipe wooden kitchen cutting boards. Baby oil tends to be cheaper but often has a fragrance added. Paraffin oil also works and can be found in hardware shops.

Water

Food colouring

Plastic dip container (clean and empty – these are the best option due to their depth)

Liquid detergent

Optional: Pipettes (if your food colouring does not come in a squeeze bottle)

Method

1. Partially fill your container with oil to about 1 cm.

2. Squirt a few drops of different food colouring randomly in container. Try to keep the different colours apart at this stage. The water-based food colouring drops do not mix with oil and will remain circular. Some individual colours may fade and turn dark blue or black. Other colours, such as green and blue, may appear black immediately on contact with the oil.

3. Gently swirl the dish to see all of the colours merge into black droplets of varying sizes.

4. Raise the container on one edge by sitting the base on a marker, crayon or a thick pencil. You will notice that the food colouring drops fall and combine. After 10 to 15 minutes, all of the droplets will have formed one large black drop (all individual colours are lost). Shake and swirl the container, and you will see lots of small droplets scattered throughout the oil again, in a range of different sizes.

Investigation

5. Allow the single large drop to re-form. This time squirt some detergent in the middle of the colour drop and observe what happens. The detergent will spread the coloured drop outwards. Swirl the container to thoroughly mix the oil, food colouring (water) and detergent. You will see small droplets appear throughout the container.

Extension

To gain a more in-depth understanding of why some liquids do or do not mix, research the following terms and concepts:

- miscible and immiscible liquids
- the structure of water, fat and detergent molecules
- what other liquids do not mix with water but mix with oil.

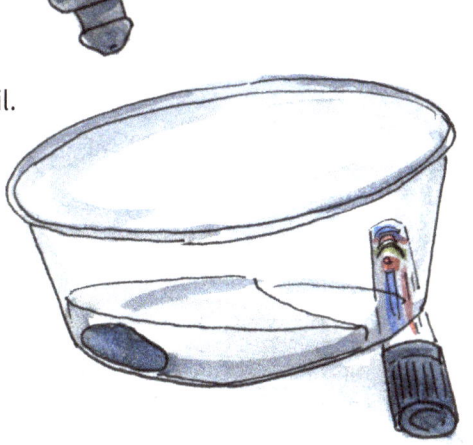

Changes to soil temperature

You may have investigated the effect of mulch on the temperature of the soil (see page 36 of *Life in a garden*). This involves measuring the temperature of the soil at a particular time each day and comparing the results.

In this investigation, you will measure the temperature of various soils over the course of one or more days.

Materials

2 ice cream containers (2 L variety)

3 L sand or garden soil

½ L mulch (e.g. shredded plant material)

2 thermometers

1 bedside lamp (You may need one on a tall stand)

Method

1. Place half of the sand or soil in each container.

2. Add 25–30 mm of mulch to one container (on top of the soil). The other container has bare soil.

3. Carefully insert a thermometer into the middle of each container to about two-thirds deep (not to the bottom). The thermometer should support itself in the soil, but you may need to rest it against the container wall or prop it somehow.

4. Place the lamp so that it will light (and heat) both containers evenly.

5. Wait two minutes, and then take the initial temperature of both containers.

6. Turn on the lamp and take the temperature reading every half hour (if you can) or hour until the end of school. Turn off the lamp and conduct the activity again the next day to build up a set of results.

7. Record your results in a table. Plot a line graph of the results and discuss your findings.

Prediction

_____
_____
_____

Results

Time (hours)	Temperature bare soil (in °C)	Temperature mulched soil (in °C)
0 (Initial)		

Investigation

Observations
_____
_____
_____
_____

Conclusions (Was the prediction correct?)
_____
_____
_____
_____

Discussion
Whenever scientists undertake experiments, they usually repeat them several times. Why do you think they do this?
_____
_____
_____
_____

Investigation

Causes of erosion

Erosion is the movement of soil by the action of running water or wind. This causes considerable damage to farmland and agricultural production. However, there are ways to minimise erosion and the loss of topsoil. To demonstrate erosion you can set up this simple investigation.

Materials

1 smaller tray or cardboard milk carton

Scissors

Clean sand

1 large baking tray or plastic tray

Small blocks of wood

1 watering can

Water

Mulch

Method

1. To make the smaller tray from the milk carton, cut off the top and one long side to leave three sides and the base.

2. Place sand in and across the smaller tray.

3. Support the sand tray at an angle (place on blocks) into the larger tray, which will collect any washed sand and water. The steeper the tray, the greater the erosion.

4. Use the watering can to wash water over the surface. Observe any sand movement and water being collected in the larger tray.

5. Repeat the procedure but place a 2 cm layer of mulch over the sand. Observe any differences between mulch cover and bare sand: is the amount of sand and water collected in the large tray the same or different? It is important to make sure that the volume of water and the rate of application is the same for bare sand and the tray with mulch.

Investigation

Further investigations and discussion

1. Research ways to minimise erosion on farms. This may involve plant cover and green manure crops, various earthworks, minimal till and the use of various soil amendments.

2. Do this experiment with different soil types. You may get a different rate of soil loss if you use fine sand as opposed to coarse sand or loam (which contains some clay).

3. Compare different mulches – organic (shredded plant materials) or inorganic (such as small stones), or coarse or fine. Try applying the mulch to different thicknesses and compare the results.

4. If there is time to prepare this, plant seeds (any) in a tray of sand, then water the seeds and keep them alive until the seedlings are 5 to 10 cm tall. This will ensure some root growth, which will help to hold the soil together and may minimise soil loss.

PART 4
Animals in the garden

Needs and uses of animals

Needs of animals

To survive, animals need oxygen (air), water, nutrition (food), shelter, appropriate temperature range, habitat (living space), and companionship and mates.

Most animals cannot survive more than a few minutes without oxygen, a few days without water and a few weeks without food. Adverse temperatures can quickly shorten the chances of survival. While a habitat may offer shelter and protection from predators, it is simply the space where they live. Their habitat can change, as some animals migrate to different areas or have a large home range.

As animals cannot make their own food, they either eat plants (herbivores), eat other animals (carnivores) or have a diet of both plant and animal material (omnivores).

Some animals are cold-blooded (ectothermic), meaning that their body temperature changes with the surroundings and they are often less affected by temperature fluctuations. Other animals are warm-blooded (endothermic), and their body temperature is maintained at a fairly constant stable state. However, rapid changes and temperature extremes of heat and cold will kill all animals. Some warm-blooded animals hibernate in winter to avoid these extremes.

While some animals live isolated or alone, all of them come together to reproduce. Some animals live in herds, some in family and extended family groups, while others are dominated by male or female leaders.

Both plants and animals are classified as living things. All living things can respire, grow, produce waste (excretion), move (even plants can make small movements of leaves and flowers), respond to their environment (organisms are sensitive to changes in the surrounding environment) and reproduce. All also have the ability to adapt to their environment.

Uses of animals

Animals have many functions in their environments. In ecosystems, all animals are part of food chains and food webs. They may also provide manure for plant growth, pollinate flowers, break down dead organisms (detritivores, scavengers, decomposers), disperse seeds, help some seeds germinate, live in close associations with other animals or plants (symbiosis), and aerate the soil. Without animals each participating in an ecosystem, the system can become unbalanced and suffer.

Humans also use animals in many ways. Animals are used for food as part of our food chain. They also provide us with materials for clothes and items for our homes, such as wool and leather. Animals also help us in gardens and farms to reduce weeds, carry loads, plough fields and control pests. They help us to connect with one another, such as pigeons carrying messages or horses and donkeys transporting us where we need to go. They also make excellent companions and pets.

Needs and uses of animals

All living things have particular needs so that they can survive in their environment. The needs of plants and animals are similar, but there are some differences too. They also have a variety of different uses, both in their natural habitat and in the wider community.

Directions

Complete this activity in pairs. One student should begin by reading the first question and listing one answer. They should then explain their answer to their partner. They then pass the sheet to their partner, who does the same, listing another answer and then discussing it. The sheet should go back and forth until all questions are answered.

1. Animals have essential needs that must be met if they are to survive. What are some of these needs?

   A. _____

   B. _____

   C. _____

   D. _____

   E. _____

2. In what ways do animals and plants differ?

   _____
   _____
   _____
   _____

3. In what ways are plants and animals the same?

   _____
   _____
   _____
   _____

4. Both plants and animals are classified as living things. How do living things differ from non-living things? (What characteristics are common in all living things?)

   _____
   _____
   _____
   _____

Science in a Garden by Ross Mars I Reproducible

Activity

5. Animals have many functions in the environments in which they live. Can you think of some functions that animals perform?

   _____
   _____
   _____
   _____
   _____
   _____
   _____
   _____
   _____
   _____

6. Humans also use animals to help make work easier. What ways do humans use animals to make work easier and save us energy and effort?

   _____
   _____
   _____
   _____
   _____
   _____
   _____
   _____
   _____
   _____
   _____

Animal products and functions

Directions

This activity can be completed individually or in small groups. Select an animal through students calling one out, selecting from the animal list or drawing from a hat. Once the animal is chosen, students have two minutes to write down all the products they can think of that come from that animal. These can be physical products such as meat, milk or wool, or could be extended for older students to include services or functions such as transport, farm work or companionship.

The student who chooses the animal should read out their list. This list can be noted on the board or on a large piece of paper for display in the classroom. Students should be encouraged to share any items on their list that haven't already been said by another student.

If there is an answer that someone does not agree with, teachers should encourage students to explain their reasoning. This could lead to a wider class discussion.

This process continues until all products and functions have been added to the list. Go through each of the animals until they have all been played.

Extension

This activity may also be completed with animals and ecosystems in mind, having students note down the ways that animals serve or play their roles in their specific environment.

Animal list

Duck	Goose	Chicken
Alpaca	Llama	Yak
Cow	Goat	Sheep
Fish	Pig	Horse
Bees	Turkey	Emu

Animals in schools

Having animals in schools and school farms raises issues about their welfare (health and wellbeing), the likely spread of disease and the provision of appropriate food, housing, pens and other structures. Government legislation protects even small animals such as rabbits, guinea pigs and mice that may be kept in a classroom. Schools usually have an animal ethics committee in place to approve the keeping of animals in classrooms and on the school grounds.

Animal ethics committees

Discuss with the class or your group what you think the role of an animal ethics committee would be and write some of these ideas here.

_____
_____
_____
_____

Animals in the classroom

What do you think would be some of the problems and issues that need to be considered if you were to keep animals in a classroom?

_____
_____
_____
_____
_____
_____
_____
_____

Activity

Animals in farm schools

What do you think would be other considerations for keeping larger animals, such as cattle and sheep (livestock), horses and pigs, in farm schools?

_____
_____
_____
_____
_____
_____
_____
_____
_____

What animal is that? bingo

Directions

Students should be provided with different bingo sheets (p. 89–91). Each bingo sheet contains common products from animals. Many of these products come from many different animals, so students will have different ways to play with their bingo cards.

The animal list (p. 85) should be cut up and placed in a container to be drawn out like bingo numbers. As animals are drawn, students should assess their bingo card and write the name of the animal into the square that shows the product that animal makes. For example, a student could write 'chicken' into the square that says 'eggs'. In some instances, there may be many different products that the animal could fit into. Students can only use the animal for one square, so should choose wisely to increase their chances of completing their bingo sheet.

When a student has completed their bingo sheet and called 'Bingo!', they must show the class that their answers are correct.

Activity

What animal is that? bingo cards

Eggs	Meat	Hair
Wax	Wool	Feathers
Honey	Milk	Manure

Science in a Garden by Ross Mars | Reproducible

Activity

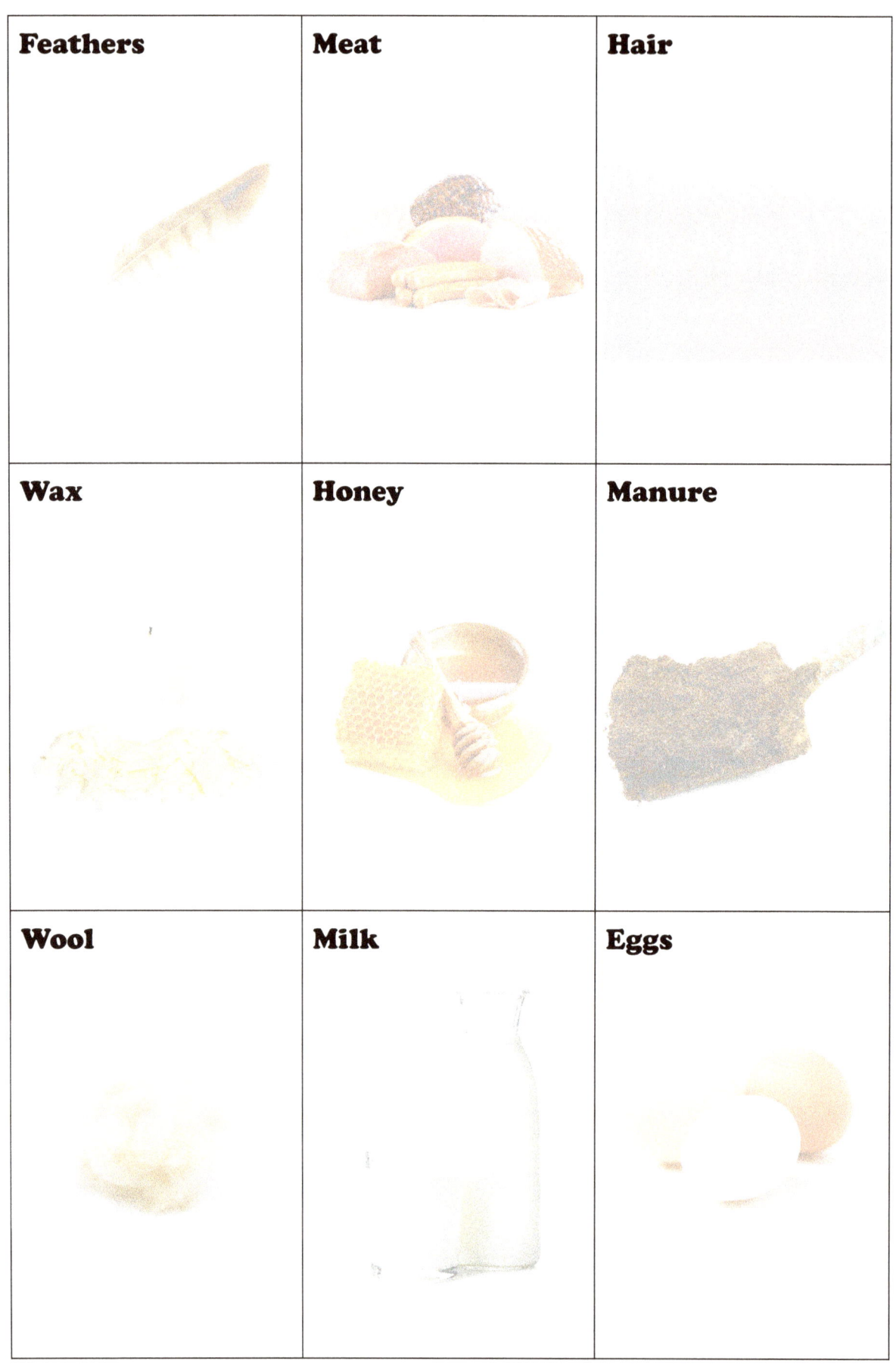

Feathers	Meat	Hair
Wax	Honey	Manure
Wool	Milk	Eggs

Activity

Wool	Meat	Hair
Manure	**Eggs**	**Feathers**
Honey	**Milk**	**Wax**

Activity

Adaptations

Adaptations are features that help organisms survive in their environment. They can be features about the size and shape of the plant or animal or the behaviour that helps them catch food, keep out of the hot sun or survive in freezing conditions. Here are some examples:

Birds and bats have a similar pattern of bones to enable them to fly.

Bears hibernate (deep sleep) to escape extreme cold in winter.

Some trees, like this bottle tree – a variety of kurrajong – store water in their trunks.

Activity

Here is a microscopic view of a leaf. The leaf openings, shown as doughnut shapes, can close in the heat of the day. Tiny hairs also keep the plant cool and protect it from harsh conditions.

Seed pods protect the developing seeds so that they can mature before being released.

Tendrils are long threads that twine around objects to enable some plants to climb upwards and support themselves.

Humans have adaptations too. What features do we have that help us live?

_____
_____
_____
_____

Science in a Garden by Ross Mars | Reproducible

Visit the plants that are growing in the school garden. Observe their features and discuss some of their characteristics below.

Plant name	Special features

Choose a common house (domestic) pet. What features does this animal have?
_____
_____
_____
_____
_____
_____
_____
_____

Adaptations in garden animals

Many animals that visit our gardens have features that provide ways for them to better survive in their environment. Write down what beneficial features these animals have under each picture. Not all of these animals may be found in your area, so you may need to do some research.

 **Bandicoot**	 **Pygmy possum**	 **Chuditch**
 **Bee**	 **Ant**	 **Wasp**

Science in a Garden by Ross Mars | Reproducible

Activity

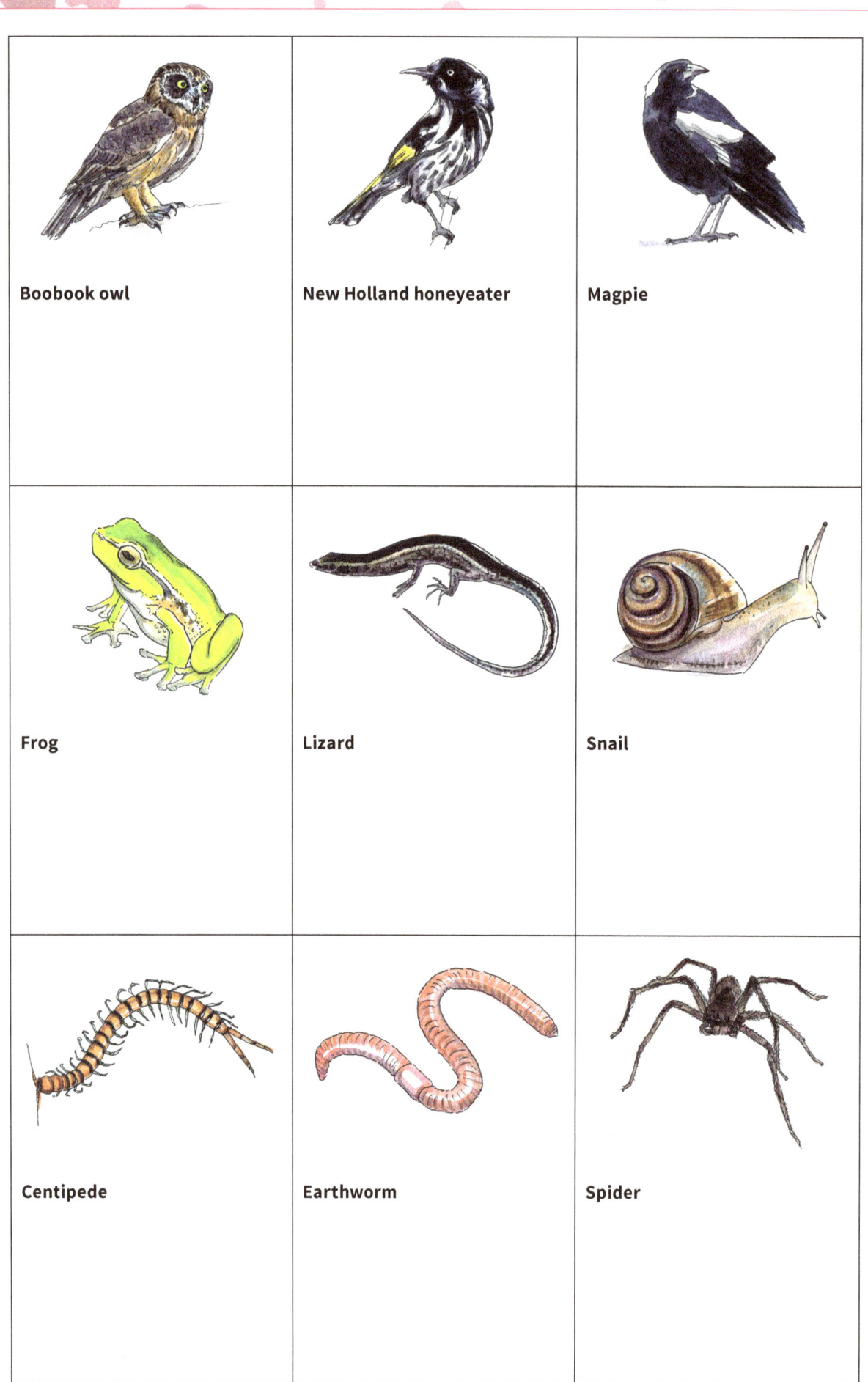

Activity

Nocturnal animal adaptations

Australia is a country of extremes. During summer the daytime temperature could be over 40 degrees Celsius, while night-times can be near freezing, and rain may not fall for months so water can be limited.

Some animals prefer to be active at night when conditions are more favourable to move about, retain moisture and obtain food. However, vision may be limited, predators can also be active at night and food may be still hard to find. Let's discuss some of the special features that animals have to survive under these conditions.

A gecko has large eyes that can see colour at night. This is quite unique because most animals cannot see colour at night. The gecko has a lot more colour and other receptors that are sensitive to dim light.

The large eyes of the boobook owl are forward facing, and they cannot move in any direction. If the owl wants to see something to one side they have to move their head in that direction. An owl can turn its head 270 degrees – nearly all the way around!

Teacher notes

The large ears of the kangaroo can each rotate 180 degrees, so they can point in different directions. This enables them to pick up sound from any direction, which is important if you want to detect and escape from predators such as dingoes.

Dingoes have very sensitive noses, and they can smell for food in the ground as well as pick up scents from animals they may be hunting.

Teacher notes

Bats use echolocation (sonar) to find food (their prey). They send out high-pitched soundwaves that bounce off objects and other organisms. They can detect the returning echo and locate potential food. Sonar stands for 'sound navigation and ranging' and is also used by other animals such as dolphins and whales to locate fish and other types of food.

Possums have a special layer of cells, called the *tapetum lucidum*, behind the retina of the eye. These reflect light back through the retina, increasing the light available to the photoreceptors, thus contributing to superior night vision. When you shine a torch into the eyes of nocturnal animals, you often see red or occasionally orange or yellow. The red colour is the reflected light coming back to the viewer.

Teacher notes

Exploring nocturnal animal adaptations

While it is difficult for students to undertake an activity on nocturnal adaptations, other than a research assignment, here are some suggestions.

1. Students work in pairs. One student carefully shines a torch into the eyes of another student to observe how the pupil will constrict and then enlarge when the light is taken away.

2. One student stands in the middle of the classroom. They will act as the predator, closing their eyes and facing one direction. Other students form a circle around the perimeter of the classroom. Get students at random to clap their hands once and ask the predator to turn and point in the direction of the sound. Repeat this as many times as you like and allow other students to be predators. How accurate were students at pointing to the source of the sound?

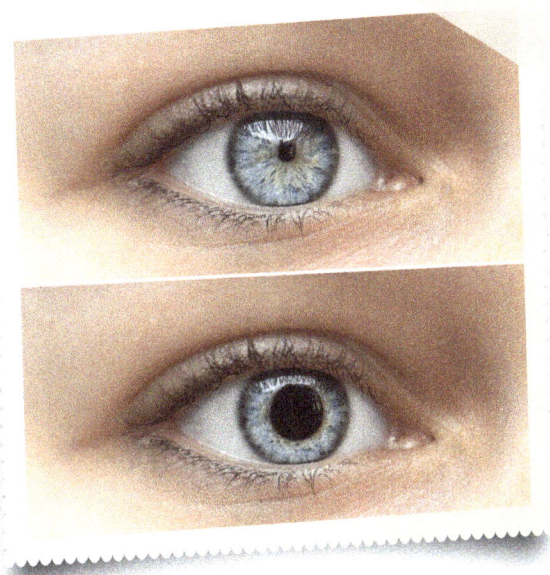

3. A variation of the preceding activity is to use a group of four or five students to demonstrate predator–prey action. Again, one student is the predator, but this time they can move about with their eyes closed. You need a clear space for this activity to avoid any injuries. The other four students are positioned around the predator. The predator claps their hands once and one prey claps twice. The predator is allowed to move towards the prey two steps at a time. The predator claps again, and the same prey claps twice. The predator can take two steps towards the prey until eventually the predator meets the prey. That student sits down with the rest of the class and another prey student takes over. Repeat the activity until all of the prey has been caught. How challenging was it for the predator to use just hearing to capture prey?

4. The predator–prey activity can also be set up to have the predator responding to a particular smell rather than a sound. Teachers can shake a bottle of perfume, place it in a desk, open the lid and ask the predator to use their sense of smell to move towards the perfume. Teachers should make sure the student doesn't knock the desk and perfume over.

Background

Mouthpart adaptations in insects

Every animal has specialised mouthparts to exploit both their particular food source and their feeding style. About three-quarters of all animals are insects, and as insects cause considerable damage to our food plants and the other plants we grow, their study helps us learn ways to combat excessive numbers of the pest insects.

Insect mouthparts are essentially divided into two main categories: chewing and non-chewing. These are then further divided into six basic types: biting and chewing; piercing and sucking; siphoning; chewing and lapping; sponging; and rasping and sucking.

Biting and chewing

Many insects have jaws or mandibles that enable the insect to grasp their prey, bite, crush and chew plants or other small animals.

In carnivorous chewing insects, such as dragonflies, grasshoppers, cockroaches and wasps, the mandibles are often serrated and knife-like, with piercing ends. Useful predatory insects, such as the tiger beetle, antlion (larvae of lacewing), assassin bug, dragonfly and praying mantis, have these types of mouthparts. In herbivorous chewing insects, such as the caterpillars of moths, mandibles tend to be broader and flatter to enable grinding and chewing. The adult forms of moths and butterflies do not have chewing mouthparts; only the larvae (caterpillars) can eat solid food. If you see holes or chewed edges of leaves, that pest has jaws.

Piercing and sucking

Mosquitos, aphids and biting midges have mouthparts that pierce the skin of an animal or surface of a plant to enable them to suck blood or other fluids such as plant sap.

Carnivorous insects, which feed on other insects or animals, include sandflies, assassin bugs and female mosquitoes. Both male and female mosquitoes feed on nectar and plant fluids, but a female mosquito also feeds on blood to make her eggs develop.

Other insects, such as aphids, mealy bugs and leafhoppers, are herbivorous and feed on plant fluids. They digest the sugar and protein in the fluids found in leaves and stems. They have to drink so much fluid to obtain enough protein for their growth that they often secrete a sugary fluid that is readily acquired by ants and other insects.

Siphoning

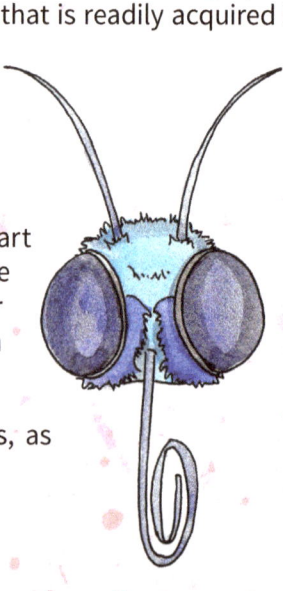

Moths and butterflies possess a proboscis, which is a long-coiled mouthpart that enables them to suck up nectar from flowers. They do not pierce the fruit or flower as the mosquito does. The proboscis is kept coiled under the head and unravels to form a tube to suck up nectar, just like when you sometimes use a straw when you drink.

Only adult moths and butterflies possess these types of mouthparts, as their larvae or caterpillar stages have mandibles to chew plant matter.

Background

Chewing and lapping

Honey bees have modified mandibles that are not serrated but blunt, and this helps them mould wax to make honeycomb. Their jaws are also used to chew pollen and turn it into bee bread, which is stored in the honeycomb cells. The pollen is used in the hive to feed young bees.

When bees move from flower to flower some pollen is caught on their bodies. They use their legs to clean their bodies, and the pollen grains are placed in their pollen sacs, or baskets, on their legs.

Bees also have a tongue that enables them to lap up the watery nectar, which they change into honey. Nectar is rich in sugars and provdes an important food source for many animals. Predatory wasps feed on nectar and, while they are in the garden, capture pest insects, which are used as food for wasp larvae.

Sponging

Some insects can only feed on liquids. Houseflies, blowflies and fruit flies do not have mandibles, so they cannot eat solids. Their speciaised mouthpart has a sponge-like end that is able to channel liquids towards its mouth and into its gut. The housefly secretes saliva onto food, and this helps to soften and dissolve it so that it can be absorbed and drawn up as a liquid.

Some other flies do possess biting mouthparts. Horseflies are a common biting pest on stock animals and humans, and tsetse flies can spread sleeping sickness throughout Africa when they bite humans.

Robber flies are predatory and they have a short, stiff proboscis, which pierces their victims. Saliva is injected into their prey, paralysing them. They can then feed on the prey's partly digested body.

Robber flies are useful predators of pests in the garden.

Rasping and sucking

Thrips and mites use their mouthpart to scrape the surface of a leaf to expose the internal cells and sap of the plant. They suck up these fluids and chloroplasts that ooze from the plant, making parts of the leaves and flowers dry out, die and finally turn brown or a silvery colour.

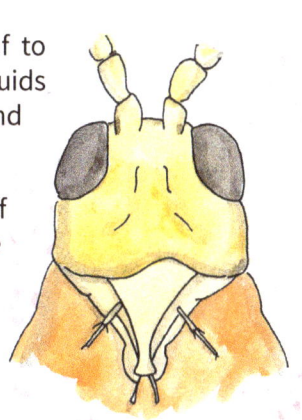

Thrips are small, slender insects, while mites belong in the spider group of arthropods as they possess eight legs. Mites are mentioned here because they have similar mouthparts to thrips and cause damage to our crops and food. Some thrips have small wings, but all thrips are light and easily blown by wind so that they can move from plant to plant. Thrips can also transfer diseases. However, not all thrips are pests. Some species pollinate rainforest plants, and some predate other insects.

Activity

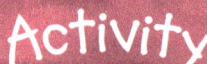

How do these insects feed?

Examine the insect head diagrams below and indicate whether they feed by biting and chewing; siphoning; chewing and lapping; piercing and sucking; sponging; or rasping and sucking.

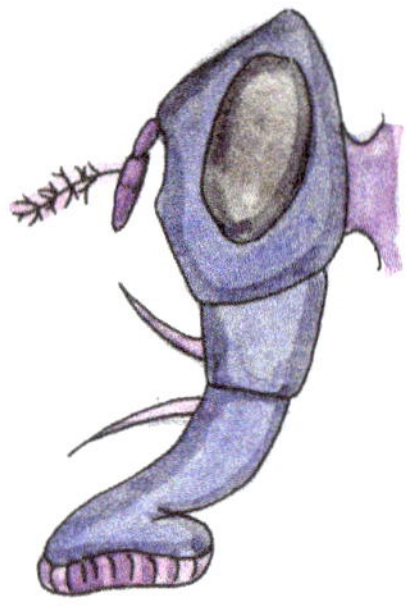

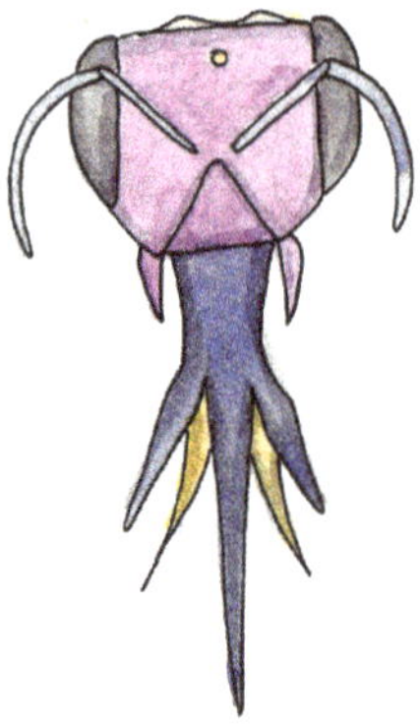

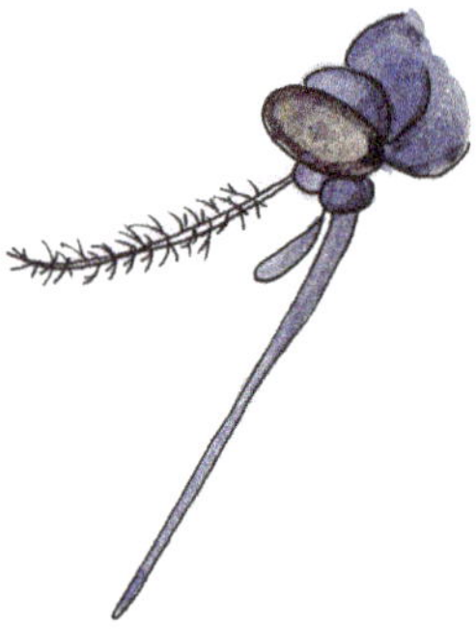

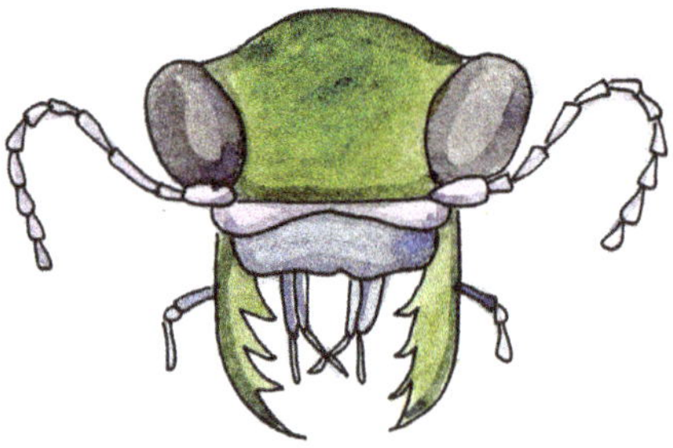

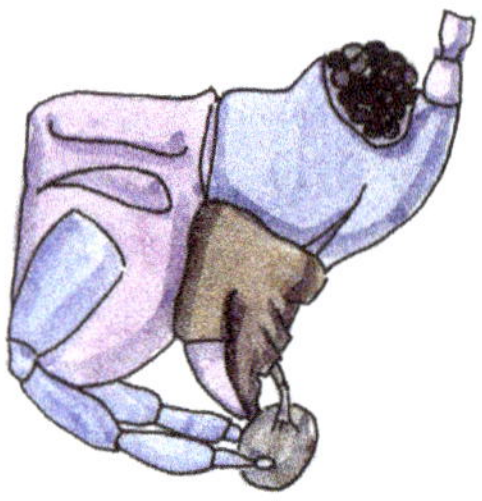

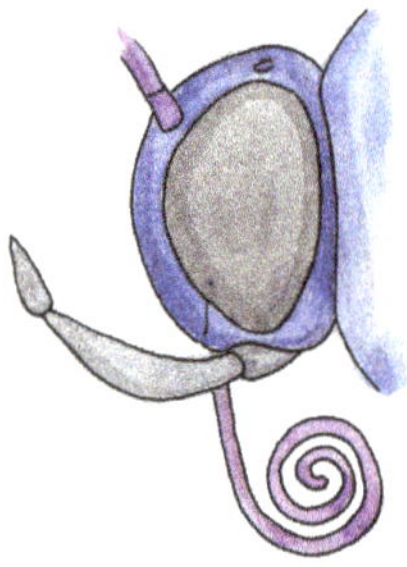

Investigation

Pollination

Pollination is term that describes the transfer of male sex cells, or pollen, to the female sex cells in a flower so that seeds form. Pollination can occur by wind or by animals. Wind-pollinated flowers are usually small and inconspicuous, while animal-pollinated flowers are typically colourful, fragrant or full of nectar to attract insects, birds or mammals. The shapes of pollen grains will provide a clue about how they are transferred. For example, if they are flat they may be carried by wind, or if they have hooks these can attach to an animal's skin or fur.

The activity on page 105 shows microscopic images of some pollen grains and students are asked to sort them into wind-pollinated or animal-pollinated plants. You can also show what real pollen grains look like through setting up the following simple demonstration.

How to germinate pollen grains

If you have access to a microscope, this is an easy demonstration to show students microscopic pollen grains.

Materials

A selection of flowers that clearly show the bright yellow pollen on the stamens

Microscope

Microscope cavity slides and coverslips

Sugar solution (10%)

Eyedropper

Large pin or needle

Method

1. Use the eyedropper to place one or two drops of sugar solution on a cavity slide.

2. Use a pin or needle to scrape pollen from the stamens into the solution.

3. Place a coverslip over the solution and leave the slide for at least half an hour.

4. Place the slide under a microscope and record what you see. Not all pollen will germinate, so you will be able to observe the initial shape of the pollen as well as notice some tube-like growth in others. If possible, use a digital microscope, which can also be connected to a computer and projector, to enable everyone to see the pollen grains.

Activity

Pollination

1. What is meant by *pollination*?
   _____
   _____
   _____
   _____

2. Examine these microscopic images of pollen grains and decide whether you think they are wind pollinated or animal pollinated. Place each letter labelling the pollen grain in the appropriate column.

Wind pollinated	Animal pollinated

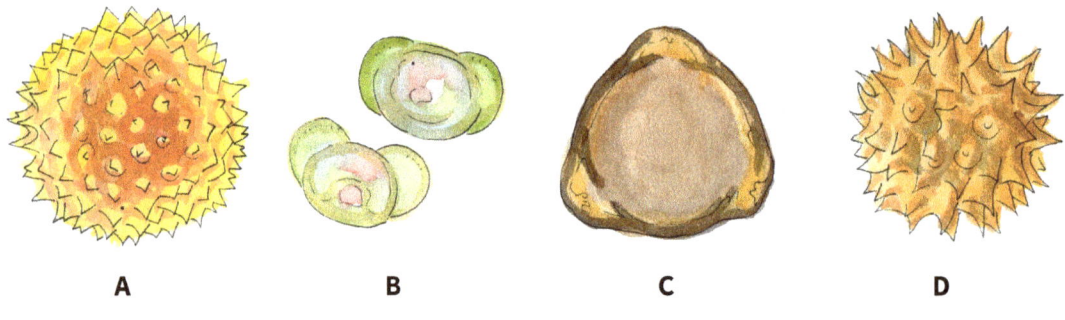

A   B   C   D

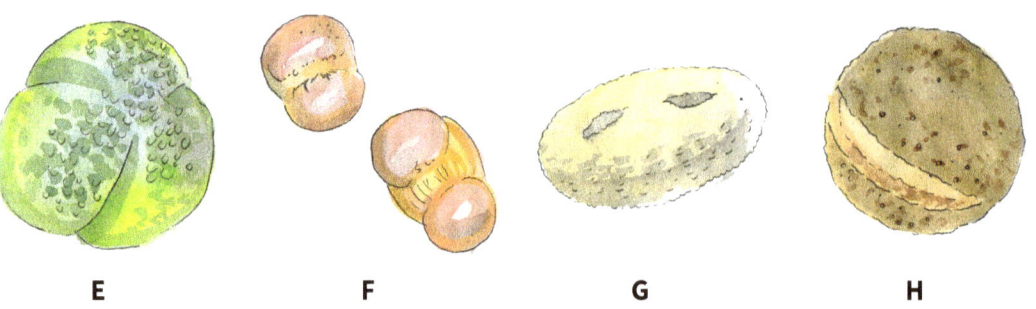

E   F   G   H

Activity

3. Explain the reasoning behind your choices in question 2.
   _____
   _____
   _____
   _____
   _____
   _____

4. Find and examine photographs of animals visiting flowers. What adaptations do these flowers have to attract pollinators such as bees, birds, small mammals and butterflies?
   _____
   _____
   _____
   _____
   _____
   _____

5. Wind-pollinated flowers have different adaptations. What observations can you make about plants that use wind to transfer pollen?
   _____
   _____
   _____
   _____
   _____
   _____

Examples of wind pollinated plants

Science in a Garden by Ross Mars I Reproducible

Background

Adaptations in bees

Bees have a variety of adaptations that help them survive and thrive in their environments. When bees forage on flowers, they collect two main things: nectar (juice) and pollen. Most prominently, bees have adaptations that help them to collect, store and spread pollen.

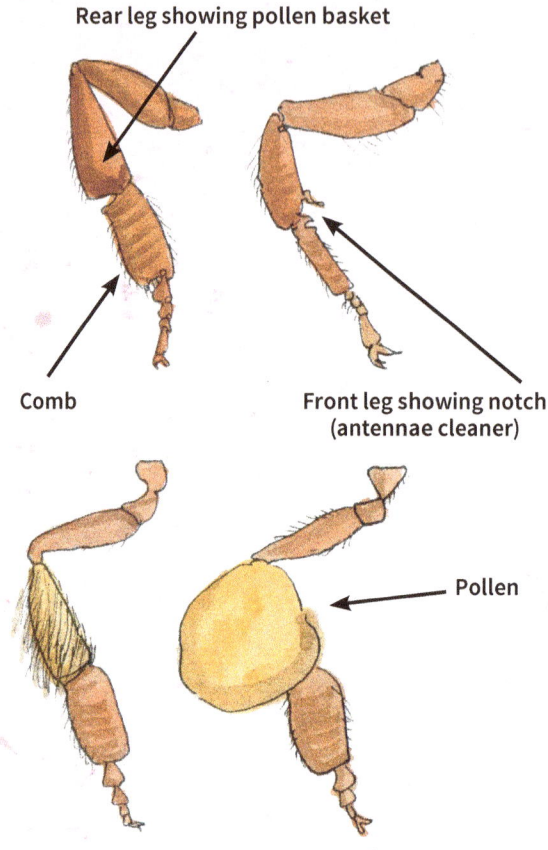

Like all insects, bees have three pairs of legs. The legs have claws to grip onto flowers, tiny taste receptors on the leg tips to enable bees to sense food sources and tiny hairs over the surface so that they can trap pollen. They use a notch in their front or foreleg to wipe pollen from their antennae, and pollen is placed in a pouch on their hind or rear leg. When the pollen basket is full, they fly to the hive where pollen is used to feed the young.

Bees flap their wings at a rate of about 200 times per second! That is one busy bee. Not only does this make them fast flyers, but it also generates static electricity. When a bee lands on a flower, the pollen is attracted to the electricity and sticks itself to the bee. The bee is then able to clean itself and collect this pollen to store it away.

Bee covered in pollen (electrostatic attraction)

Bee cleaning antennae

Background

A bee tongue can lap up nectar from a flower. Nectar is a sugar-rich solution that ultimately makes honey. The bee stores the nectar in its stomach to bring back to the hive then spits it out to begin the production of honey. Bees also use their tongues to collect a resin-like substance from some trees, which is called *propolis*. This is used to seal their hives and fill gaps so predators cannot enter. Bees also make wax, which is secreted from special glands in their abdomens. Bee wax is used to make the honeycomb walls that store the honey.

The distinct colouring of bees is also an adaptation. The yellow and black stripes help the bees in two ways. Firstly, they help the bee to camouflage when they are gathering pollen, making it harder for predators to spot them. Secondly, these colours can intimidate predators when the bees are spotted. The colours black and yellow are an indicator that an animal may be a threat or poisonous. This helps to protect the bee and ward off any potential dangers.

Bee tongue to lap up nectar

Colour (stripes) for camouflage

Sting for protection of hive

Adaptations in bees

Introduce students to adaptations in bees through the background information provided on page 108. This should give students the foundational information about adaptations in bees that will allow them to answer the questions in this activity.

This is a four corners activity. For this activity we suggest having corners labelled *protection*, *collecting pollen*, *storing pollen* and *collecting nectar and propolis*. You can then ask students questions that allow them to identify which of these roles certain adaptations serve. For example, what is the main benefit of the black and yellow colour of bees? Students will go to the corner that represents their answer.

If students go to a variety of different corners, ask them to discuss with their group why they think they are in the right corner. Then have the groups explain their discussion to the class. This could show that there is more than one right answer, or some students may change their minds and switch corners.

Extension

Students can research how bees make wax and how it is used to make honeycomb, and the role of propolis in the hive.

Australian native bees

Bees collect pollen from flowers, which they use as food. If you have read about bees, you will know there are plenty of ways that a bee's body helps them to collect and transport this pollen. In this activity, you will research Australian native bees and their adaptations. You may wish to research bees you have seen in your school garden.

To encourage native bees in your school grounds, you can make a bee hotel, and this is described in *Life in a garden* (p. 63).

A native bee entering its nest hole

Research the special adaptations of Australian native bees and record what you learn.

_____
_____
_____
_____
_____
_____
_____
_____

On a blank sheet of paper or on the back of this activity sheet, draw some of the Australian native bees you could expect to find in your area.

Activity

Butterflies

Butterflies have a long narrow tube in their mouth, called a *proboscis*, that acts as a straw. They usually sit on top of a flower and drink the nectar. Nectar is a sugary solution, and this provides nourishment. Find out about butterflies and some of their features and describe these below.

Find out about some of the features of butterflies and how they differ from other insects.

_____
_____
_____

Go out into your garden and see if you can find some butterflies. Colour in the template below based on your observations of butterflies in your garden.

Write down some of your observations about butterflies you find in the garden.

_____
_____
_____

Science in a Garden by Ross Mars | Reproducible

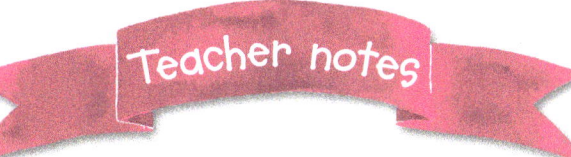

Adaptations in birds

All animals have adaptations to enable them to obtain food and other resources and to survive in their environment. Birds have many characteristics that enable them to perch or scratch, fly through the air and catch prey or eat particular foods. Their beaks have different shapes and sizes as adaptations for that species. Examples of bird beaks and what they foods they are suited to are shown below.

New Holland honeyeater – sucks up nectar   **Duck – filters water**   **Cockatoo – cracks hard seed pods**

The terms *bill* and *beak* are synonymous, and they refer to the bird's modified mouthpart that is used to capture and eat food. Birds do not have teeth, but some have serrations and various shapes that suit the foods they eat. Long and pointed beaks are used to suck up nectar, small insects and other creatures living in water. A duck's beak is often called a bill because it is fleshy. The wide bill sifts food out of water, and this is a common feature of wading birds. Birds with thick, strong beaks with a slight hook tend to crush seeds and break up fruits, seed pods and nuts. These types of foods are eaten by cockatoos, galahs and parrots.

Kingfisher – spears fish, grubs and insects   **Eagle – tears meat**   **Robin – crushes insects**

Birds that have long but sharp pointed beaks tend to spear their prey, such as insect grubs, fish and shrimp. Birds of prey, such as hawks, eagles and owls, all have curved beaks that enable them to tear flesh. They are carnivorous and eat small mammals, lizards, snakes and fish.

Short, robust beaks are used to crush either small insects or seeds. A robin eats insects while finches and sparrows eat seeds. Some birds that eat insects that have to search under bark have longer and thinner beaks.

Activity

Adaptations in birds

Examine each of the beaks of these common birds and make suggestions about what kinds of foods they might eat. Complete the table provided with your observations and thoughts.

Twenty-eight parrot

Chicken

Black honeyeater

Spoonbill

Sandpiper

Willy wagtail

Brown falcon

Goose

Red-browed finch

Activity

Bird	Features of beak	Kinds of foods they might eat
Twenty-eight parrot		
Chicken		
Black honeyeater		
Spoonbill		
Sandpiper		
Willy wagtail		
Brown falcon		
Goose		
Red-browed finch		

Extension

1. Using the internet or books from the library, learn about the feet of birds. Assemble pictures or create some drawings of the different types of feet and write about what their feet are adapted for.

2. Examine the adaptations and features of birds in more detail. Research what characteristics they have that enable them to fly or grab fish from the ocean or run like an emu.

Adaptations in common animal garden pests

Slaters, snails, slugs and caterpillars are common garden pests. Snails and slugs are both molluscs (like mussels and oysters), and slaters are crustaceans (so they are related to crabs and prawns). Butterflies and moths are known as caterpillars during their larval stage. Caterpillars generally eat leaves, but some, such as the codling moth and the cluster caterpillar, eat fruit.

These garden pests are all found on land, whereas most molluscs and crustaceans are found in water. Most molluscs have shells to protect them, but the slug has tough internal tissue, called a mantle, to protect it from predators. Slaters have their own characteristics that enable them to survive in their environment. They can roll into a ball so that their hard shell is on the outside. Caterpillars are often coloured to blend into their surroundings.

The following simple demonstration will enable students to observe common garden pests in greater detail and make observations.

Materials

Glass sheet (so you can see underneath how they walk or slide)

Sawdust, coffee grounds or wood ash (other coarse materials work too)

Copper wire or plate (available from many hardware stores)

Garden pests (Not all pests are available all the time, so you might need to see what is available.)

Method

1. Provide students with the worksheet on page 118. You may want to provide multiple copies of the worksheet if you are able to find several pests to examine.

2. Place a snail, slater, caterpillar or slug onto the sheet of glass. Students can lift up the sheet and examine the animal from below, noting how the animal moves.

3. Put sawdust, coffee grounds or wood ash in their path and observe their reaction.

4. Try a piece of thick copper wire or a section of copper plate on the glass sheet. Again see how each animal behaves.

Observe slugs, snails, and caterpillars (shown) from underneath the glass sheet

Teacher notes

Copper provides a natural barrier to some organisms

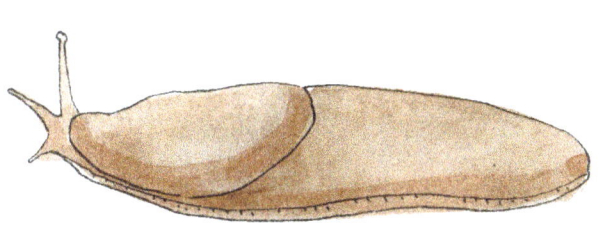 

Snails have a shell while a slug has a tough mantle to protect it

 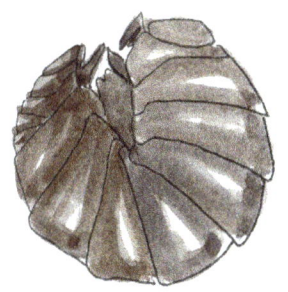

Slaters are land crustaceans. When touched they roll into a ball

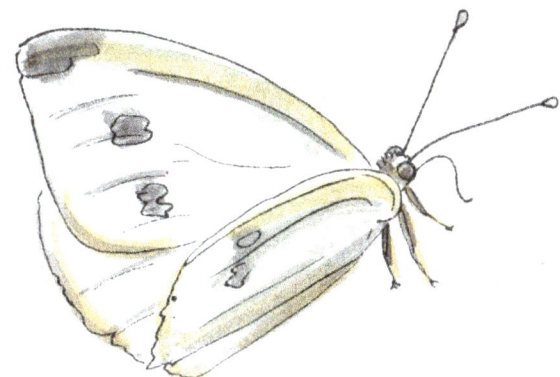 

Students may be able to observe white butterflies flying around the garden, but examining caterpillars is easier as these are easily captured. You or students may be able to use a net to catch adult butterflies and bring these back in the classroom, but it would be better if these were dead specimens.

Adaptations in common garden animal pests

You are to observe a few common garden pests, such as snails, slugs, caterpillars or slaters. Examine these to determine their special features that enable them to survive in their environment. Make some sketches and notes in the spaces provided.

Animal: _____

Adaptations

_____
_____
_____
_____

Animal: _____

Adaptations

_____
_____
_____
_____

Background

Predators in the garden

Pests are organisms that cause problems in the garden. Some pests eat the food we grow. We should try to minimise the damage that pests cause to our food crops.

While some pests can be controlled by chemicals, there are many other ways to minimise pest damage that are safer for us and the environment.

Every pest has natural predators. Examples of predators include lizards, who eat snails and slugs, frogs, who eat mosquitoes and other flying insects, and ladybirds, who eat aphids.

We can encourage predators into our gardens so that they eat the pests. Water in the garden is important to attract predators. All organisms need water, so putting a pond or water trough in our gardens will provide a drinking source for predators, attracting birds, lizards, dragonflies and other predator insects like wasps and hoverflies.

Some types of flowers are important to attract predators. The flowers provide nectar or pollen, which predators can also eat. When birds visit the garden they may also eat grubs and other insects.

To attract predators into the garden you may also need to provide shelter to protect the animals. Piles of logs and stones are places where lizards can hide. Aquatic plants near a pond enable frogs to hide, and nesting boxes may encourage birds to visit and live in the garden.

Many animals are helpful predators. Spiders often trap flying insects, and some wasps lay their eggs inside a pest. However, some insects are not helpful. For example, some types of ants can carry aphids from one tree to another and so spread the pest throughout the garden. Putting grease in a ring around the lower part of the stem stops the ants from climbing the tree.

Predators in the garden

Research how these organisms are used in pest control in the garden. Explain in one or two sentences in the space provided.

Organism	How it is involved in pest control
Frog	
Lizard	
Ladybird	
Spider	

Activity

Organism	How it is involved in pest control
Wasp	
Bird	
Bird of prey (owl, hawk, eagle)	
Marsupial carnivores (chuditch, quoll, Tasmanian devil)	

Activity

Your garden ecosystem

Part 1

Have students observe animals and insects in the garden, noting down what each animal does, how it interacts with others and what role that animal may play in the garden. Each student should be encouraged to observe a different animal or species, if possible, to gather information on a variety of creatures in the garden ecosystem.

Alternatively, you may assign a common garden animal or insect to students and have them research their assigned animal. To complete the second part of the activity students will need to understand how their animal or insect engages with others in the garden ecosystem.

Part 2

For this part of the activity you will need a ball of string long enough to be passed around the group and name tags to identify the different animals that each student will represent.

Once the observation or research phase is complete, have students stand in a circle. They should each wear the label of the animal that they have observed or researched. You should also have an animal name tag and start with the ball of string. Holding onto the loose end of the string, throw the ball to a student and explain how your animal interacts with the student's animal. That student then continues the process by doing the same and passing the ball along to someone else. The ball of string should be passed around until every student has been included in the garden ecosystem.

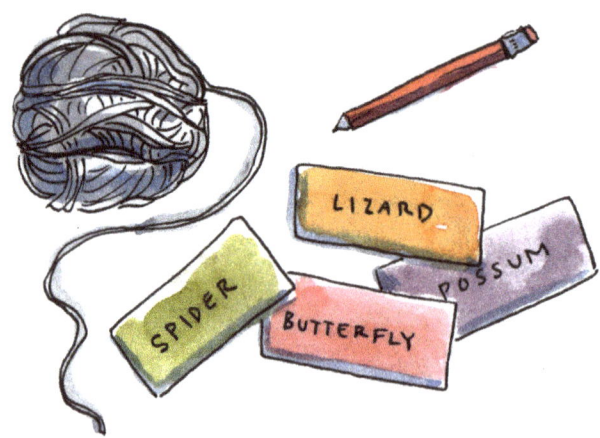

Activity

Extension

Once all students have been included in the ecosystem, you may wish to turn the game into a wider discussion. You may wish to pose questions that explore how changes in balance or habitat may affect the ecosystem as a whole. You may wish to have students step outside the circle to show the gaps if one species is threatened or removed from the ecosystem.

This activity could also be completed with a variety of other habitats and ecosystems to show that all ecosystems rely on every creature, big or small.

Background

Pest control

Besides using natural predators, we can do many things to minimise pests. Using sawdust around plants stops slugs and snails from eating your vegetables, sprinkling flour over cabbages and broccoli will discourage the green vegetable grub, and hand-picking snails and slugs will reduce their numbers and the damage they can cause. Simple sprays using garlic or chillies will also repel many pests.

Not all pests in the garden are insects or other animals. Disease organisms, such as bacteria and fungi, also affect our plants. These microorganisms can infect the leaves and fruits of plants making them rot.

While there are few natural predators that will eat fungi and bacteria, we can use many strategies to reduce the effects of these pathogens. For example, making a solution of sodium hydrogen carbonate (known commonly as bicarbonate of soda or bicarb soda) with a small amount of oil and detergent in a bucket of water and then spraying it on the plants helps reduce the effects of moulds and other fungi on the leaves of plants.

Making sure the plants in our garden are healthy will help them resist the effects of pests and disease. Plants need regular fertilising and care, and the occasional seaweed extract spray will strengthen their defence mechanisms.

Strategies for pest control

- Introduce natural predators, such as frogs for caterpillars, predatory wasps for small insects, ducks for snails and slugs, for natural pest control.

- Encourage natural predators into your orchards and gardens through mixed planting. For example, buckwheat attracts hoverflies. These beneficial insects predate on aphids, leafhoppers and mealy bugs.

- Choose the placement of herbs and other plants carefully through companion planting to maximise the benefits of each plant.

- Practise sound management and husbandry to discourage soil and leaf pests. For example, remove fallen fruit, cover composting material and use crop rotation.

- Use plant-derived sprays to control or repel insects and other pests, fungi and viruses, such as pyrethrum, wormwood, nasturtium, garlic and chamomile.

- Use plant competition to control land and aquatic weeds. For example, pine needles inhibit weed seed germination.

- Employ insect traps and behavioural chemicals (lures), including fruit fly baits and beer for slugs and snails.

- Use mechanical management strategies and barriers, such as hand-picking off insects and snails, creating sticky or wet bases of fruit trees to discourage climbing insects, placing sawdust around garden beds to discourage slugs and snails, and using diatomaceous earth to cause dehydration of an insect's body.

Background

- Try specific biological pest control, such as fungus or bacteria, to kill pests. For example, DiPel is a bacterium (*Bacillus thuringiensis*) that only kills caterpillars.
- Use attractants and food to induce predators into the garden, including water sources, blossoms and nesting boxes.
- Select disease-resistant stock and rootstock for the main fruit crops.
- Learn about specific crops to attract certain animals. For example, trap crops, such as dill, attract tomato hornworm, and hyssop attracts white cabbage butterflies.
- Use natural chemical control, such as sulphur or neem oil.

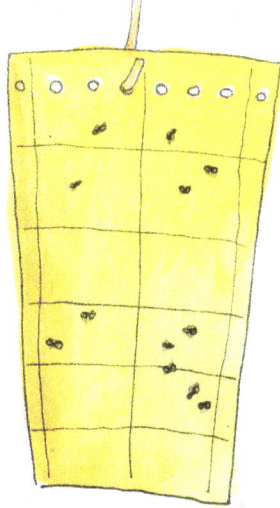

A sticky insect trap

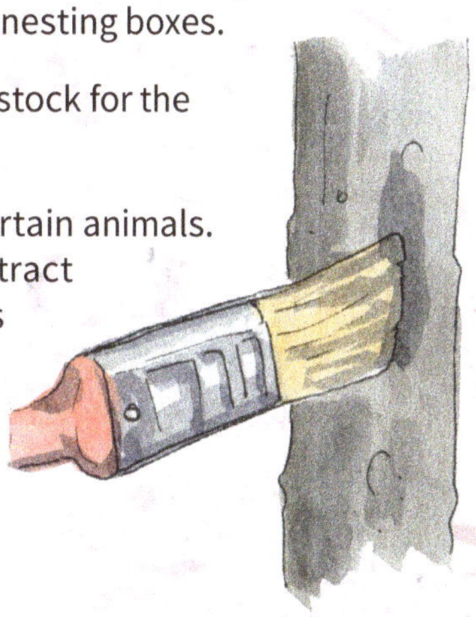

Paint oil or grease on plant stems to stop insects and other pests from climbing upwards

Use water and plants to attract predators into the garden

Activity

Soil critters

In leaf litter and the first few centimetres of soil, you can usually find large numbers of animals and organisms, including earthworms, insects and mites, nematodes, fungi, bacteria, land crustaceans and single-celled protozoa. These feed on the organic matter present and on each other.

Microscopic life

Most of the organisms that live in soil are only visible through a powerful microscope. These include bacteria and single-celled algae. Bacteria, like fungi, are decomposers, and they cannot make food themselves and must feed on other organisms or organic material. Decomposers break down dead organisms (both plants and animals) into simpler substances that can ultimately be made into complex substances and used by another organism to survive.

Organisms larger than bacteria are called *microfauna*, and this includes single-celled organisms, such as protozoa, and simple organisms, such as rotifers and minute flatworms. All of these move about the soil and feed on other microscopic life.

Single bacteria cell (such as *Escherichia coli*)

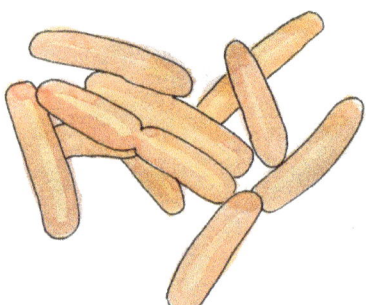
A colony of *Bacillus bacteria*

Fungi (toadstools)

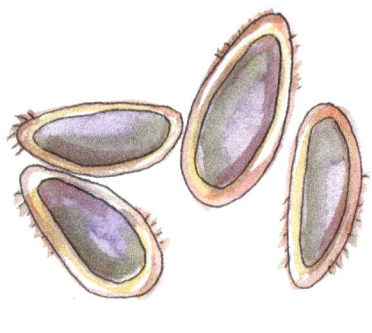
Protozoa (e.g. paramecium)

A protozoan (such as a rotifer) showing part of its flagellum

Mycorrhizal fungi

Macroscopic life

These organisms may be small, but they can be seen with your eyes. The smaller organisms in this group are the *mesofauna*, and these include nematodes, mites and springtails.

Macrofauna are even larger again, common examples being ants, termites, slugs and snails, millipedes and centipedes, insect larvae, and various beetles. These feed on decaying matter, other organisms and plants.

Finally, the largest soil organisms are called *megafauna*, and these include earthworms, burrowing animals and fungi.

Fungi tend to be large and visible to the naked eye, such as mushrooms and toadstools, but some have microscopic threads, such as the mycorrhizal fungi, which help plants obtain water and nutrients in exchange for food.

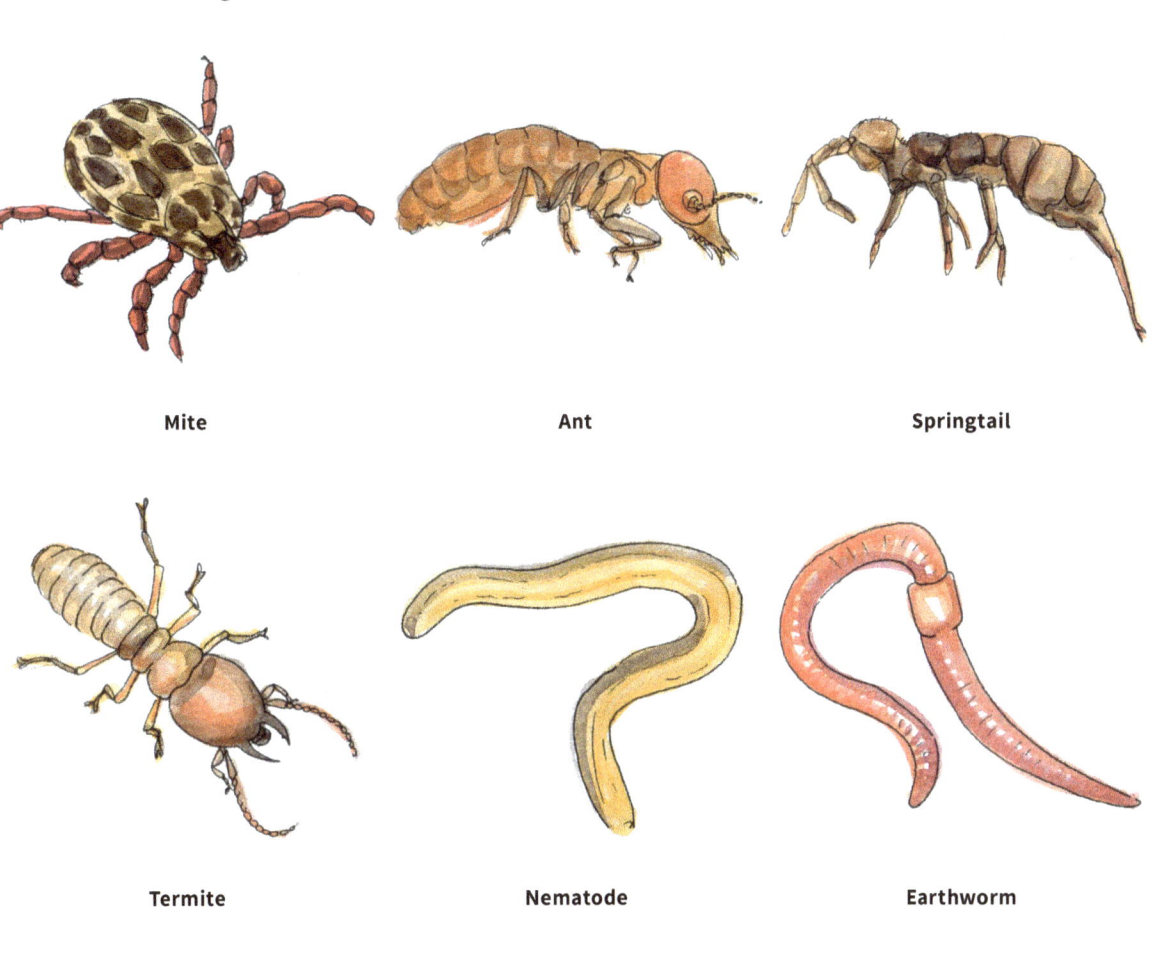

Mite   **Ant**   **Springtail**

Termite   **Nematode**   **Earthworm**

Activity

1. Which organisms are decomposers?
   _____
   _____
   _____

2. Which organisms are producers in most environments?
   _____
   _____
   _____

3. What is the original source of energy for producers?
   _____
   _____
   _____

4. What role do termites play in the soil?
   _____
   _____
   _____

5. The majority of organisms in the soil and compost are microscopic. What does this mean?
   _____
   _____
   _____

PART 5
Human use of the garden

Investigation

Bush medicine plants

Australian native plants contain particular substances that may help to fight disease. First Australians have been using extracts from plants for thousands of years to treat a range of illnesses, skin conditions and other ailments with great success.

Some examples of native plants that are used in medical applications include tea tree oil (*Melaleuca alternifolia*), which is used as an antiseptic to kill bacteria, fungi and other disease organisms, and kangaroo apple (*Solanum aviculare*), which contains a steroid that is important to the production of cortisone. Cortisone helps relieve inflammation, pain and swelling.

Science has also discovered that emu bush (*Eremophila spp.*) is also antibacterial, native apricot (*Pittosporum angustifolium*) has been shown to have antibacterial and antifungal properties, and the sap (latex) of native figs (*Ficus spp.*) can kill warts and fungal skin infections.

In this activity you are to use tea tree oil or eucalyptus oil to examine its effects on microorganisms. The aim is to capture spores from the air that will grow into colonies of bacteria and fungi. You can recognise bacteria colonies because they are generally shiny dots, whereas fungi tend to grow as irregular fuzzy or furry patches.

Materials

10 g agar or gelatine powder

Tea tree oil or eucalyptus oil

Petri dishes (at least two per student or group)

Sticky tape

Native apricot

Method

1. To make agar or gelatine plates for the whole class, use 10 g agar to 1 L water, or one sachet of gelatine (10 g) to 500 mL water. Heat the water to near boiling and stir in the powder to dissolve. One litre of solution should be enough for about 50 petri dishes (25 students or groups).

2. Divide the solution into two. In one half add 50 mL of your selected oil and stir.

3. Pour both solutions into separate petri dishes. Label the lids of dishes either *C* (for *control*) for plain agar solution or *A* (for *antiseptic*) for the oil solution.

4. Place the lids over the dishes and allow to cool and set. Each student or group should have at least one of each dish.

Investigation

5. Expose each dish to the air for 20 to 30 seconds. Replace the lid, use sticky tape to secure the lids so they can't be opened, place the dishes in a warm, dark place, and allow the fungi and bacteria to develop.

6. Check the plates in a few days. You may have to wait a week before growth can be seen. Record your observations over the next week or two.

7. Don't open the lids because there may be potentially harmful microorganisms in the culture. After the experiment is complete, place all dishes in a sealed bag and dispose of it in the bin.

Prediction
___
___
___
___

Observations
___
___
___
___
___
___
___
___

Conclusions (Was the prediction correct?)
___
___
___

Dispose of this experiment properly

Activity

Nutritional value of bush foods

Australian bush foods have been found to be very nutritious. While many of these are edible, only a few are palatable. This means that the majority of bush foods don't taste that nice. Even so, plant foods have historically composed up to 80 per cent of the diet in desert areas and up to 40 per cent in coastal areas.

Bush tucker is generally low in energy density but high in nutrient density, being high in protein, low in sugars, high in fibre and high in micronutrients. The carbohydrates have a low glycaemic index value, producing lower glucose and insulin levels than similar Western foods. Their consumption may be protective against diabetes.

As one example, research has found that the green plum in northern Australia (Kakadu plum – *Terminalia ferdinandiana*) contains about 3000 milligrams (per 100 grams) of vitamin C – making it the richest source of vitamin C in the world. This is 30 times more vitamin C than goji berries, 60 times that of oranges and over 300 times that of blueberries.

Kakadu plum

Directions

Examine the tables that follow and answer the questions in the spaces provided.

Table 1: Nutrient content of bush foods compared to the common tomato and fig

Plant	Energy (kJ)	Protein (g)	Fat (g)	Carbohydrates (g)	Thiamine (mg)	Vitamin C (mg)
Fig (common)	311	1	0	19	0.01	2
Sandpaper fig	548	4	0.8	29	0.13	234
Desert fig	569	3	2.1	36	0.1	2
Tomato	76	1	0	4	0.1	19
Bush raisin	570	3.8	0.6	32	0.21	19

Note: Values listed per 100 grams of food.

1. What general comments can you make when the nutrient content of common figs is compared to sandpaper and desert figs?

_____
_____
_____
_____
_____

Science in a Garden by Ross Mars | Reproducible

Activity

2. What general comments can you make when the nutrient content of the common tomato is compared to the desert tomato – the bush raisin?

_____
_____
_____
_____
_____
_____

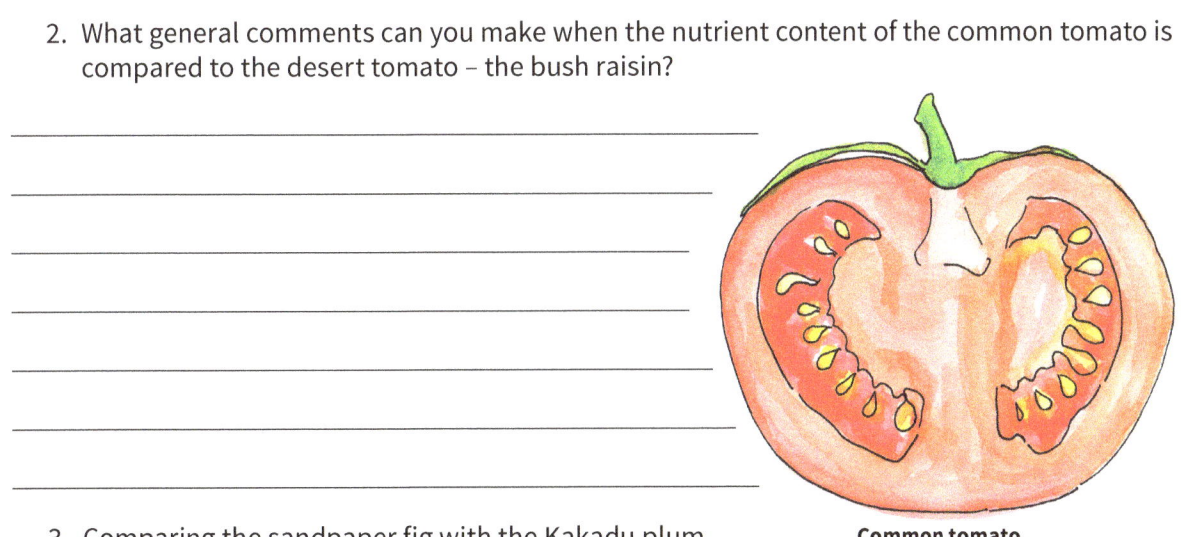

Common tomato

3. Comparing the sandpaper fig with the Kakadu plum, approximately how much more vitamin C is found in the Kakadu plum? Use the space below to show your calculations.

Table 2: Nutrient and mineral content of bush foods compared to the common plum, almond and pecan nut

Plant	Energy (kJ)	Protein (g)	Fat (g)	Carbohydrate (g)	Vitamin C (mg)	Iron (mg)	Magnesium (mg)	Calcium (mg)
Plum	193	1	0	10	9.5	0.35	12	10
Quandong	335	2.3	0.2	21	ND	0.5	34	53
Sandalwood	636	3.3	4.4	26	15	1.9	55	41
Almond	2286	21	30	21	0	3.5	255	251
Pecan	2900	9	72	14	1.1	2.5	121	70
Macadamia	3015	8	76	14	1.2	3.7	130	85

Note: Values listed per 100 grams of food.

4. Of plum, quandong and sandalwood, which do you think has the overall highest nutrient value? Explain your answer.

_____
_____
_____
_____
_____

Science in a Garden by Ross Mars | Reproducible

Activity

5. Compare the data for pecans and macadamias. Pecan nut trees originate from North America while macadamia nut trees were originally found in northern New South Wales and Queensland. Which nut do you think has the highest nutrient value? Explain your answer.

_____
_____
_____
_____
_____
_____

6. Examine Tables 1 and 2 and compare all fruits and nuts listed. Why do you think nuts, generally, have higher energy and nutrient content (such as protein, fats and some minerals) than fleshy fruits?

_____
_____
_____
_____
_____

Almonds

7. What role does each of the following play in plant structure and function? You will have to undertake some research to find out about these substances.

   (a) Protein _____
   _____

   (b) Fat _____
   _____

   (c) Carbohydrates _____
   _____

Extension

Learn about the nutritional value of peanuts.

Peanuts

Science in a Garden by Ross Mars | Reproducible

Growing a bush food and bush medicinal garden

A list of common bush foods can be found in *Life in a garden* (p. 124). Some mention of common bush medicines is made in the activity on page 128 of that book. Students will need to source information about appropriate native plants to grow in their particular soil and climate.

This activity has two parts. First, students should research and select plants that can survive at their school. While you can buy rainforest bush food plants that originate in northern New South Wales and Queensland, they may not tolerate the drier, harsher conditions found in country and outback areas.

Many bush food and bush medicine plants are known about but are simply not available because few nurseries grow these types of plants. If you find it difficult to source these plants, you can select local grevilleas, bottlebrushes and banksias, which are a source of food through the nectar in the flowers. The seeds of many wattle trees can be ground to make flour, and the gum that oozes out of the stem is usually edible too. Source endemic acacia species to help fill the garden space. If the school has enough space, various eucalyptus and other large trees can be planted. The leaves and gum of some eucalypts have cultural significance to First Australians.

Second, students can plan, design and plant their native garden. Once plants have been chosen to suit the soil and climate of your area, work with students to design the planting regime. They will have to place plants according to height, spread and whether they tolerate partial shade or prefer full sun.

Designing the garden space

You will find some relevant information about designing school gardens in *Life in a garden* (p. 2). You will learn some of the things that work in schools, what needs to be considered when setting up a garden space and how children can be involved.

Preparing the soil

All native plants have adapted to their surroundings. Many can exist in almost pure sand, some like a little bit of clay, and others exist in loamy soils. Some amendments to existing soil may be necessary to change the pH of the soil or to address known nutrient deficiencies, such as adding compost or fertiliser. Organic matter is essential to soil life and to plant growth, but just 2 to 5 per cent organic matter content in the soil is all that is required to grow food. Don't add too much compost, other organic matter, fertiliser or amendments to the hole when planting.

Individual garden beds

While you can put all types of plants in one garden area, sometimes it is better to plant them in themes or plant them according to their water requirements. For example, bush food could be in one area and bush medicines in another, or all plants that suit dry, sandy conditions could be placed together and watered appropriately, while rainforest plants that might require higher humidity, richer soils and frequent watering may be better placed together.

Teacher notes

Planting out

There are many differing ideas about best practice for planting. The following are some suggestions that seem to work well.

- Don't remove the pot or tube until you are ready to plant. Exposed roots will dry out quickly and may damage the plant.

- Soak the whole pot in a bucket of water for a couple of minutes. This saturates the soil, providing enough moisture reduce any setbacks (shocks to the plant) when planted.

- Dig a hole deep and wide enough to easily contain the pot with space on all sides. This allows loose soil to be carefully placed while the backfilling around the roots. If the soil needs amendments and compost, these can be added without the hole being filled too much. However, don't make the surrounding soil too rich as this may discourage roots from growing outwards in search of nutrients and water.

- Gently squeeze and tap the pot so that it is easier to slide the plant out. Larger pots can be placed on their side to help their removal. Sometimes a good thump on the pot is useful to enable roots to pull away from the pot wall. Rotate the pot and tap each side in turn.

- Inspect the root ball after the pot is removed. If the plant is root-bound and the roots seem to be traveling around the outside, they will need gentle teasing out. You want the roots to grow downwards and outwards rather than around and around. If you find that some roots need cutting away and the root mass is thus shortened and damaged, consider cutting the leaf part as well. What damage done to the roots is balanced with similar damage to the leaves and branches.

- The general practice of planting is to make sure the top of the root mass (soil in pot) is level with the ground. However, it is possible to bury the plant deeper to cover the lower part of the stem. In many instances this will encourage root development in the covered area and may contribute to greater survival rates.

- While the plant stem (trunk) doesn't have to be placed centrally in the hole, do make sure it is vertical.

- When backfilling the hole, gently push the soil against the root mass. This ensures good contact between the roots and soil and removes large air pockets.

- Don't stand and stomp around the plant to compact the backfilled soil. This could damage surface (feeder) roots.

Place a layer of mulch around every tree and shrub

Teacher notes

- If the plants are on a slope, make a small berm (ridge or bank) in an arc on the downward side to catch any run-off water.

- Always water the plants once they are in the ground. Let the water soak in, add some more, and repeat. Ideally, the whole root ball and surrounding backfill is saturated. Depending on the season and rainfall at the time, you may need to water the plants every few days to get them established.

- Don't add any fertiliser during planting. Wait at least a few weeks before this is undertaken. Often you can leave fertilising for six months or more. Let the plants overcome the shock of the planting procedure first.

- Always cover the soil with mulch. Any mulch will do! Mulch can be applied 30 to 50 millimetres thick.

Maintenance of plants

All plants require maintenance. This may mean occasional fertilising, regular watering, yearly pruning, removal of weeds and re-topping the soil with mulch. Different plants have different requirements, so make sure these are known and carried out.

First Australians and the environment

You are to research how First Australians have traditionally used plants and animals and interacted with all aspects of their environment. You may wish to research the First Australians peoples of your local area and focus on their culture.

How have First Australians traditionally used these materials in their environment?

Plants	Animals
Fire	**Soil and rocks**
Water	**Ores and minerals**

How have First Australians traditionally responded to different habitats and seasons?

Desert areas	Coastal areas
Changes in the seasonal climate	**Types of tools used**

Earth pigments

Natural pigments can be sourced from a wide variety of materials in our local areas. They can be found almost anywhere. Often the colours match the landscape, with earthy and sandy shades the most common. Brown pigments are very common; haematite is a reddish-brown ochre, and limonite is a yellow iron oxide. Some of these are heated to form variations of colour that range from pale yellow through to dark reddish-brown. The most common-coloured ores in Australia are those of iron oxide. However, in other countries, there are some stones that produce colours we are more used to painting with. Lapis lazuli was commonly used to make blue, and malachite can be used to make green.

The best places to source pigments are the banks of streams and rivers. The movement of water exposes the rocks, giving a wider range of rocks and pigments to choose from. Other good places to source pigment rocks are sites where the earth has been dug up or shifted. It is important to be careful in these areas, especially if there are uneven surfaces, exposed holes or dangerous objects. These pigments can be ground up and mixed with water or oil to make a natural paint.

First Australians ochre art

Ochre is the name given to a number of earth pigments. The use of ochre pigments has a very long tradition in Australia, and it was used in trading and transported throughout the country. Besides ochres, charcoal, white and coloured clay, and mixtures of blood, feathers, fat and other organic material were traditionally used as paints. These traditional materials were applied in several ways:

- blowing a fine spray from the mouth to produce stencils. This is common in rock art
- brushing the pigment using a stick or hair brush. This is used for decoration of rocks and implements
- applying the paint using fingers and hands. This is used in body painting.

A variety of ochres and pigments are readily available from specialist stores, art and drawing suppliers, and online. These pigments can be mixed with a little water or vegetable oil to form a paste. Place a half a teaspoon of pigment in a milk bottle cap, or another small plastic container and use a toothpick to mix with one or two drops of water (or oil). Use thin paint brushes to decorate rocks, pavers, poles and other objects that could be placed in the garden.

Project

Painting with earth pigments

In this project, you will explore the ways that paints can be made with natural pigments found in rocks and clays.

Materials

A selection of rocks and clays

Bowl or container

Water

Paintbrushes (or sticks)

Plain white paper or Australian animal templates

Optional: Mortar and pestle

Method

1. Rub two of same type of stone together over a bowl or container until the rocks begin to form a powder. Alternatively, you can crush the rocks in a mortar and pestle to get a powder.

2. Mix the powder with water until it makes a paste.

3. Dip the paintbrushes in the paint. You may wish to paint onto plan white paper so that you can compare the different colours, or you may want to colour in some Australian animal drawings. There are many different templates that can be sourced online.

Extension

- You can trial different quantities of water to make different consistencies of paint to see how this changes the colour when you paint it. What does adding more water do to the mixture? Why do you think it may give this result?

- You can mix the ochres with vegetable oil and compare the results with the water-based paints. Is a better paste made? Do the oil-based paints produce different shades of colour?

- You may wish to paint some decorations for your garden. You could paint flat rocks, bark or raised vegetable gardens to add variety to the garden. Watch the decorations over the coming days and weeks. Has the paint faded or disappeared? Why do you think this is?

Grow your own clothes

This activity enables students to grow flax and cotton, both of which are used to make linen and other clothing. They will not be making garments, but they can investigate some of the procedures used to grow, harvest and treat these plants to make the fibres we commonly wear. Also detailed here are some activities to for obtaining oils and fibres. The seeds of flax (*Linum usitatissimum*) and cotton (*Gossypium hirsutum*) can be bought from many online seed merchants, and flax seed is often available at health food stores.

Flax

Flax, also known as linseed, is an annual growing to 90 centimetres with an upright habit and blue flowers. Seed can be ground and used in cereals and breads or used to create linseed oil. The outer fibres of the stem are used to make linen.

Flax is a cool season plant that prefers temperatures of 10 to 27 degrees Celsius until the blooming stage, and then hot, dry weather is best for threshing and drying the straw. It thrives in climates with a rainfall of 450 to 750 millimetres a year, prefers a heavier, well-drained fertile soil to sand (not waterlogged) and can tolerate some soil acidity.

Germinating seed

Soak the seeds in a cup of water for a few hours. The seeds are very mucilaginous, and you might find the seed solution a little thick. Carefully pour off the water. You can wash the seeds to remove their jelly coating, but there is no need to do so. Use a teaspoon to spread the seeds over a soil tray or directly into shallow furrows in the ground. Seeds should germinate within two weeks.

Harvesting

The flowers appear 60 days after planting, followed by the seed capsule. About 80 to 100 days after planting, when the seeds are quite ripe, the plants are ready for pulling. The best time is when the seeds are beginning to change from green to a light brown colour and the bottom half of the stalks are yellow.

The plants are pulled roots and all to give the maximum length of fibre. It takes about a week in good weather to dry the plants.

Obtaining fibres

To do this properly requires a lot of time and some special tools to split the stalks, remove the central pith and separate the fibres. A simple demonstration to engage students is to pound the stalks on a flat surface with a rubber mallet (don't pulverise) and then pick out the outer fibres as best you can. There will be a mixture of long and short fibres, all of which are used to make yarn and linen.

Solvent extraction of oil

Flaxseed contains about 30 per cent oil, but the following activity is crude and usually only a few drops of oil are obtained. There is usually enough fat and oil residue that students can see the yellow oil colour and certainly smell the characteristic odour of linseed oil. Commercial extraction uses solvents such as hexane, and this is usually heated to improve oil removal. For this activity, do not heat or uses solvents that are too volatile and combustible.

Teacher notes

Materials

1 tbsp flaxseed (or more)

Mortar and pestle

Vial, with lid

A non-polar solvent (such as petrol), odourless solvent (artist oil solvent) or acetone.

> Note: You will have limited success with rubbing alcohol (isopropyl alcohol). Odourless solvent can be purchased from many artist and drawing supply stores. Acetone can be purchased from fibreglass and resin suppliers.

Paper towel

Filter funnel

Jar (to collect the solution)

Teacher notes

Method

1. Grind the seeds with the mortar and pestle. You may need to grind a small amount at a time. Persevere, as the flaxseeds are not easy to crack open. You are not making flour, but you do need to split the seed coat and contents. You could also hammer seeds to crush them (see the directions for oil extraction for cotton seed, p. 144).

2. Scrape the seeds into a vial. Just cover the seeds with the solvent. If you are using acetone, it may react with some plastic containers, so use a glass vial or a jar and metal lid.

3. With the lid on tight, shake thoroughly. Rest. Continue this process, on and off, for about 10 to 15 minutes. This will enable as much oil as possible to dissolve in the solvent.

4. Place a piece of paper towel into a funnel and filter the solvent into a jar.

5. Place the jar in direct sunlight, outside and away from students. You want the solvent to evaporate away, leaving the oil behind. Acetone and petrol work fast (they are more volatile), but odourless solvent and isopropyl alcohol take a little longer.

Extension

The flaxseed coat contains high levels of mucilage. This is a mixture of substances, such as proteins and polysaccharides, and forms a gel or sticky solution. To highlight how mucilaginous the seeds are, students can cook some seeds in water.

Grind up some seeds with the mortar and pestle, place them in a saucepan, add a cup of water and gently simmer on a stove for about 15 minutes. Students will notice a jelly substance in the water as well as a fatty oil residue floating on the surface. They would also have seen mucilage after soaking the flaxseeds in preparation for germination and planting. The seeds are held in this soft jelly mass.

Cotton

Make sure you obtain *Gossypium* cotton, not the weedy cotton bush *Gomphocarpus fruticosus*.

True cotton, *Gossypium hirsutum*, is a bushy perennial to 1.2 metres with cream-yellow to pink hibiscus flowers in spring and brown pods filled with fluffy cotton balls in summer. Commercial growers in northern Australia grow cotton as an annual because they defoliate the whole plant before the cotton bolls (ripe buds) are harvested.

Germinating seed

Place the seeds in hot water and soak for a few hours, then plant directly into trays or the ground. Seeds prefer warm climates, so you may need to grow the plants in a hothouse in cooler regions. A heat bed is ideal, but warm soil is required. Different regions in Australia have different growing seasons, so you need to learn about your area.

As with all plants, you need to fertilise and water cotton seeds. Seeds usually germinate within a few weeks but can take longer. Cotton plants need regular watering over summer.

Cotton flowers, buds and cotton fibre

Harvesting cotton

Cotton plants take four to five months for the cotton buds to mature and become ready to be harvested. Hand-pick the fluffy open buds. Separate the seeds from the fibres. The seed fibres (hairs or lint) can be woven into cotton fibre, and the seeds can be pressed for oil.

Solvent extraction of oil

Cotton oil is edible, but it contains a wide range of substances that have to be removed before it can be used for cooking or eating. In this activity, just the crude oil is extracted, and it should not be consumed. Like the flax oil activity, the return is low and often just an oily or fatty residue is all you get. Achieving a yellowish colour of the solvent is evidence for oil removal.

Materials

1 tbsp cotton seeds

Hammer and paper bag

2 jars (including 1 lid)

Solvent (odourless solvent, isopropyl alcohol – rubbing alcohol, acetone or petrol)

Paper towel

Filter funnel

Method

1. Place seeds in a paper bag and use the hammer to crack them. Pound them on a hard surface. The seeds are very thick walled and cannot be ground with a mortar and pestle. The more the seed is crushed up, the more oil can be obtained.

2. Scrape the seed pulp into a jar and just cover with the solvent. Screw on the lid.

3. With the lid on tight, shake thoroughly. Rest. Continue this process, on and off, for about 10 to 15 minutes. This will enable as much oil as possible to dissolve in the solvent.

4. Place a piece of paper towel into a funnel and filter the solvent into a jar.

5. Place the solvent solution in direct sunlight outside the classroom. It may take a few hours for the solvent to evaporate away, possibly all day, but it will leave a yellow to red oil residue behind. Using a wide-mouth jar or petri dish will enable faster evaporation.

Teacher notes

Weaving (fibre basketry)

Many fibres from your garden plants can be used in weaving, and basketry opens up another world of materials, plants and artistic expression.

Suitable plants include the leaves of cordyline, banana, dracaena, flax, gladiolus, iris, pampas grass, watsonia, dianella, gymea lily, mat rush, bulrush and sedge. The stems and twigs of willow, wisteria, grapevines, couch grass, honeysuckle and jasmine are also commonly used.

Fresh leaf and twig material is best, as it tends to be soft and pliable enough to manipulate. You may need to soak leaf material for some hours or even overnight to permit weaving to occur. Pat these leaves dry with a cloth before you start.

There are lots of books about weaving, many providing patterns and clear instructions on how to make baskets, hats and other items. Only a brief outline of three basic and common techniques is presented here.

Square weave

This is a basic weave and is used as a base for bowls, hats, baskets and mats.

Method

1. Lay leaves parallel to each other, with a space the width of a leaf between each.

2. Place a heavy piece of wood or brick on one end of your leaves set-up to keep that end still.

3. Lift up every second leaf and place a new leaf horizontally across the remaining fibres. Place the leaves back down,

4. Lift up the next alternating set and repeat the process.

5. Keep the overlapping leaves close together. It is possible to adjust the weave by pushing the fibres together to tighten it up.

6. To finish the 'square' you could sew around the perimeter to hold the leaves in place.

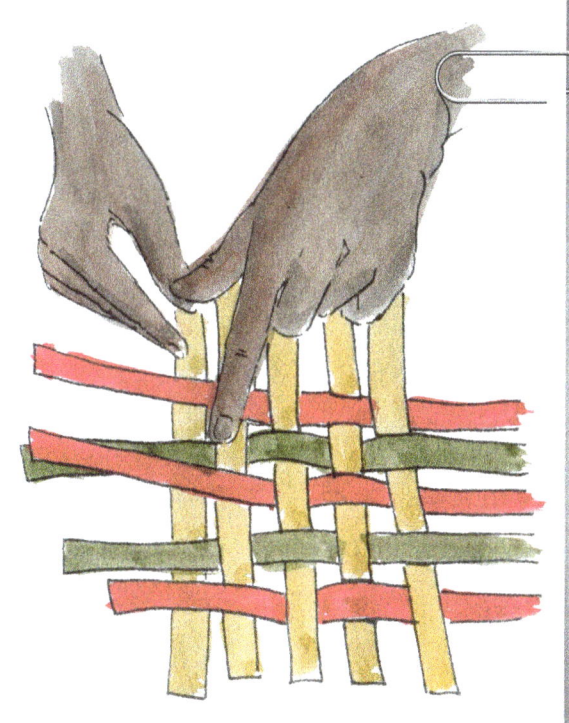

A square weave

A variation of the square weave is the diagonal weave, which adds variety to your project.

145

Teacher notes

Randing

This is a simple under-and-over weave, where fibres are wound through stakes. This weave is ideal for bamboo and brushwood fences where stem material is passed through poles.

Method

1. Place stakes or poles apart at even distances.
2. Weave the fibre through the poles, in and out. Try to keep the fibres close together and not too slack.
3. For the next layer, start the fibre in the opposite position.

Randing

Twining

Twining or pairing is a closer weave than randing. It is also an under-and-over weave, but two fibres are threaded at the same time so that they cross one another. Rushes, reeds and sedges all make good material for weaving. All three are wetland plants, and species of each type are commonly found throughout the world. Sedges are flat-bladed plants, rushes have cylindrical leaves (often with air spaces throughout), while reeds are from the grass family and include species of papyrus, *Carex*, *Typha* and *Phragmites*.

Method

1. Place stakes or poles at even distances apart.
2. Take a pair of fibres. Thread one through the poles as you did with the randing technique.
3. The second fibre starts on the opposite side of the stake and is threaded under and over the first fibre so that they cross between the stakes.
4. Once threaded, push the pair of fibres down to sit firmly on the previous weave.

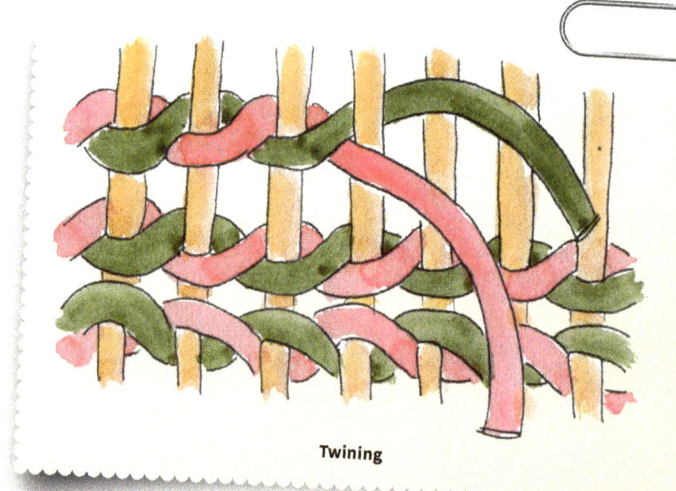

Twining

Teacher notes

Making rope from plant material

Normal rope is usually three strands of material wound around each other. This is not the same as a braid or plait, where the strands are woven together. Using plant material to make braided rope is easy. It is similar to weaving. The simplest rope is a weave of three fibres, but thicker rope can be made by using five- or seven-strand plaits. The fibres of sisal, hemp and jute are commonly used to make rope, but many other plants can be used. Long strips of flat-bladed plants such as banana, sedge, *Carex*, watsonia and dianella are suitable.

Method

1. Obtain thin strips of leaves. Cut the leaves with scissors or a utility knife along the length of the leaf. You can also learn how to extract the fibres from the bark of some types of dead trees or use animal hair instead. If you want to practise the technique before you thrust into plant braiding, just use string.

2. Tie the three strands together at one end (with a simple knot or elastic band).

3. To plait or braid, start with the left-hand strand and pass it over the middle strand. It has now become the middle strand. Pass the right-hand strand over this new middle strand.

4. Repeat this procedure until you have reached the end of the strands, leaving enough room to tie the ends together so that it doesn't unravel.

You can use this braided rope to tie your bamboo fence or poles together, make a handle for your basket, produce a bracelet or leash, or for any other types of lashings. Braiding allows you to join the leaves of onions or garlic together so that they can be hung as they dry out or stored until you need some for cooking.

Three-strand braid or plait

Braid onions together and hang to store

147

Make your own sundial

There are several ways to make a sundial, and a few examples are discussed here, starting from a simple one made from a paper or plastic plate to a wood sheet with a fancy gnomon (the part of a sundial that casts a shadow to mark the hour).

There are two ways to make the sundial work. Either you mount the plate on an angle equivalent to your latitude, or you mount the plate level (lying flat) and the gnomon is shaped to provide the angle of your latitude. The latter is the most common way, but both are shown in this activity.

A simple sundial

Materials

Paper or plastic dinner plate

Marker or marking pencil

Thumb tack/drawing pin

Protractor

Thin dowel or balsa wood
(6 mm – a straw can also be used)

Method

1. Find the centre of the plate and mark with a dot.

2. Use the drawing pin to pierce the plate at the dot.

3. Draw a line across the plate, marking the diameter. This will intersect with the dot.

4. Position the plate so that the diameter line is horizontal. From the left-hand side of the diameter line, use your protractor to mark 15° increments along the edge of the plate, using the centre dot as your vertex.

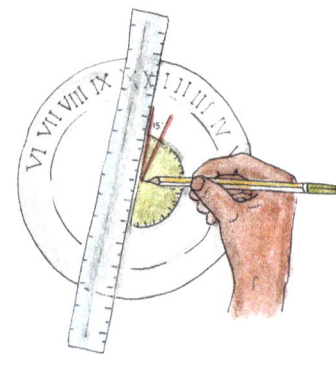

5. Label each increment as per the image shown to represent the hours of the day. You might choose to use Roman numerals or Arabic numbers.

6. The balsa wood is the gnomon. This should be about 150 to 200 mm high. Fix the gnomon to the plate by sticking the drawing pin through the bottom of the plate into the wood. Your gnomon should stand upright. If you want to use a straw, make the centre hole bigger and work the straw in so it is a tight fit.

7. For this sundial to be accurate you need to mount the plate on an angle equal to the latitude of where you live. For example, Melbourne is 38°, Sydney is 34°, Perth 32° and Adelaide 35°. You can look up any town in Australia and find out its latitude. Mounting the sundial on this angle means the sundial is parallel to the axis of the earth's rotation.

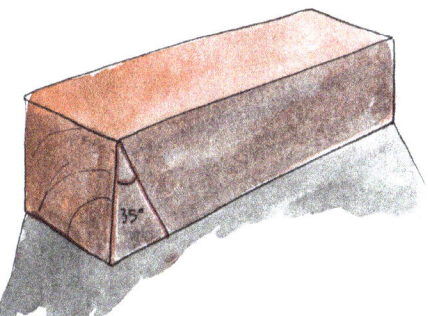

Mark the angle of your latitude to cut a pole tip or timber piece so that the plate is fixed at that angle

8. To mount the plate, you can either use a pole and cut the timber at the angle of your location or prop the plate at the angle using blocks or pinned to a piece of timber. Use the protractor to mark out the angle on the pole or timber piece.

9. If you use a pole it is fixed vertically with the angle facing north. The plate faces north with the numbers facing south. The 12-hour position is due south. Use the compass to get your bearings and position the sundial.

10. To calibrate the sundial and make sure it is positioned correctly, use a clock or watch and at 12 noon examine the sundial. The shadow should be on 12. If it is not, swivel and adjust the sundial as necessary. You can check on the shadow at other times too. Visit the sundial at 1 or 2 pm and again at 10 or 11 am.

A fancier sundial

Materials

Plywood sheet (6 to 12 mm thick)

> Note: You will need to get the help of an adult to cut the plywood for this activity.

Protractor

Marker or marking pencil

Glue (wood or PVA)

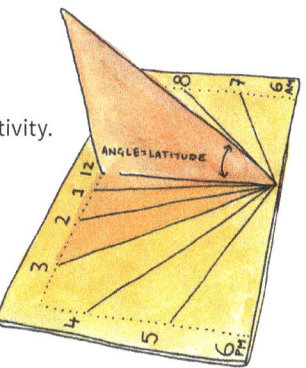

Method

1. Cut the plywood sheet either as a rectangle, square or circle about 300 mm in diameter or width. Use the method outlined in the simple sundial method to mark your hour numbers.

2. Cut another piece of plywood to make the gnomon, which should be a right-angled triangle shape. Mark out the gnomon shape with the protractor and pen, making the bottom angle match the latitude of where you live. Attach the gnomon to the sundial with glue along the 12 hour. Support the gnomon in a vertical position to allow the glue to set.

3. Mount the sundial on a flat surface. Orientate the 12 to south with a compass. Check the accuracy by seeing where the shadow lands at various times of the day by checking the hour with a clock. Make adjustments as required.

Minimising waste in the garden

Whenever we plant and work in the garden, we produce waste. This may include branches and plant material after pruning, plastic flower pots and punnets after planting, dead or diseased plants that have been removed from the garden, and plant labels, ties and small stakes that are leftover once shrubs and trees have been planted. There are many options to deal with waste or the potential to generate waste: we could reduce, recycle, re-use, rot and refuse.

Discuss with your group what you could do to minimise waste and record some ideas in the following spaces.

Reducing _____
_____
_____

Recycling _____
_____
_____

Re-using _____
_____
_____

Rotting _____
_____
_____

Refusing _____
_____
_____

Activity

Can your group think of other uses for used flower pots or seedling punnets? Write some of your suggestions here.

_____
_____
_____
_____
_____
_____

How can these materials be re-used or recycled?

Plant labels

Plastic garden stakes and trellis frames

A waste audit

School waste can include food scraps, cardboard, paper, glass, aluminium cans and a range of general waste (such as pencils, crayons, staples, and paint and artist supplies). A waste audit enables students to determine how much of each waste type they find.

In the strictest sense, a waste audit is where students will examine the contents of bins and separate the items they find. They can calculate the amount, volume or weight of each waste category to see which waste is the most common and which can be recycled or reduced in some way. These findings and ideas may contribute to the school developing a better waste management program.

Teachers can decide if they want students to inspect all waste types or just paper and cardboard and other items that are normally placed in recycling bins. While it may be messy, students will get most value in sorting all types of rubbish. You may need to send letters home to parents informing them that students will sift through bins. As long as you take precautions, such as aprons, rubber gloves and safety glasses, the risk is minimal, especially if students only sift through the bins from the current day and are not exposed to bins with food scraps and other organic matter that may have been accumulating over a few days.

Students can be encouraged to think about the large volumes of waste produced by our community that ends up in landfill, where it is typically buried. They can also discuss ways to minimise this waste and which types of items can be recycled and repurposed for other uses.

A waste audit

Materials

Aprons or protective clothes

Safety glasses

Good-quality rubber gloves (not thin disposal ones)

Sources of waste materials (bins from the canteen, school office, classrooms, schoolyard)

Large plastic sheet

20 L bins or buckets

Method

1. This activity may require permission from the principal as well as from parents for students to conduct the waste audit and to sift through bins. Ensure that you have gained all required permission before commencing the activity.

2. Discuss with students the audit and the types of waste they think they may encounter from bins around the school. Discuss any safety requirements for the activity and have students put on the protective clothing prior to starting.

3. Send students off in pairs to various places around the school to collect the bins and bring them back to a central place, such as an outside play area.

4. Spread a large plastic sheet over the ground. Place smaller bins nearby to collect each type of waste once it is sorted. You might decide to have waste separated into food scraps and organic matter, paper, cardboard, metal, glass, plastic and general waste. You could split paper further into writing paper, coloured paper and food wrappers. Plastic could also include plastic wrap or stretch film from lunch boxes. It may be interesting to see if some of the food scraps are whole, uneaten foods such as fruit or complete sandwiches.

5. Upend each bin brought to the area, sort the contents and place in the individual waste bins. You may need a larger bin for cardboard boxes. Students need to be very careful, as they may encounter broken glass and other sharp items.

6. Calculate the volume or weight of each stream. Volume could simply be calculated by students estimating how many full and partially full buckets of each waste type they have found.

7. Set up a table similar to that provided here to record the results. Choose appropriate headings. Calculate total volumes and weights so that calculations can be performed.

Audit results	Food scraps	Glass	Metal	Paper	Cardboard	Plastic	General	Totals
Volume (L)								
Weight (kg)								
Percentage								

8. From the volume or weight of each waste type and the total volume or weight collected, calculate how much of each type of waste there is as a percentage or fraction of the whole. Once data has been collected for that day, students can then work out what volume they could expect over a five-day school week and over the school year (40 weeks). This could represent the amount of waste that goes to landfill.

9. Discuss the findings with the students. Are there some waste products that can be recycled? How can students reduce the amount of waste they produce? What is the best way to deal with food scraps and other organic matter?

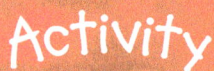

Waste audit evaluation

In this activity you will evaluate your findings from the waste audit and come up with suggestions for how to address these observations. This will be specific to your school and allow you to personalise the waste management of your school.

What are the items that are most common in your waste audit? Are they products or materials?

_____
_____
_____
_____

In groups, brainstorm ways that these common items can be reduced or re-used in your school and garden community. Record your ideas here.

_____
_____
_____
_____

Look at the bottom of any plastic items. You should see a small triangle with a number inside. Find out more about these recycling codes, including the common products for each type of plastic and whether they can be recycled. Note down what you learn in the following table.

Plastic number	Type of plastic	Common uses or products	Can it be recycled? Where?

PART 6
Products from the garden

Background

Food from the garden

Some food comes from plants.

Some food comes from animals.

Some food comes from flowers.

Some food comes from the roots of a plant.

Some food comes from fruit.

Some nuts are eaten as food.

Some swollen leaves can be eaten too.

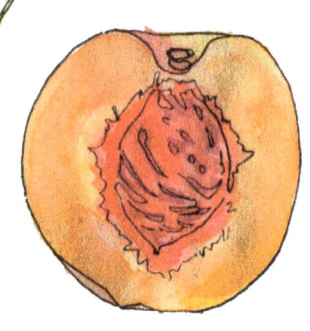

Some food comes from tubers.

Some food comes from leaves.

Some food comes from stems.

Some people eat meat that comes from animals.

Insects are small animals, and they are common in the garden. Bees, butterflies and wasps are all insects.

Bees make honey from the nectar of some flowers. Wasps help control pests.

Some people eat the products of animals, such as honey or eggs.

Some seeds can be eaten as food. You might put them in a salad.

Things that grow in a garden and that we use in some way are called *produce*.

Some produce can be changed to make a new food type. Milk can be made into yoghurt or cheese. Some fruit juices can be made into fizzy drinks.

Some foods can be made into new products. Excess fruit from the garden can become jam.

When too much food is made in a garden, some of it can be stored or dried so that we can use it later.

Using food from the garden

Using the food we grow is one of the pleasures of life. Provided we grow it organically, it is generally safe to eat. However, there will always be a few pests eating leaves or fruit and the occasional disease that infects the plant. This is why we must always practise good hygiene and safe handling procedures.

1. What is meant by *hygiene*?
   _____
   _____

2. List a few examples of things you can do to maintain good hygiene.
   _____

3. Explain, with a couple of examples, what safe handling procedures are.
   _____

Once our produce is picked, we can take it to the kitchen. Often, we need to store the produce for some time before we use it.

4. How can we prepare and store our food if we cannot use it straight away?
   _____

5. Imagine all the different types of food and produce we can harvest from the garden. List some of the ways we can use this produce.
   _____

Extension

Find out about these techniques that are commonly used to reduce waste when we have excess produce. Write one or two sentences about each.

Preserving

_____

Bottling

_____

Canning

_____

Drying

_____

Fermenting

_____

Science in a Garden by Ross Mars | Reproducible

Types of vegetables

Look at the pictures of common vegetables. Place the correct name from the list provided under each vegetable. Identify the part of the plant that the vegetable comes from. Colour in your vegetables.

Vegetables: *Carrot, spinach, asparagus, potato, artichoke, capsicum, lettuce, beetroot, cauliflower, broccoli, onion, peas.*

Plant parts: *Flower, bulb, stem, fruit, stalk, root, tuber, seed and pod, leaves*

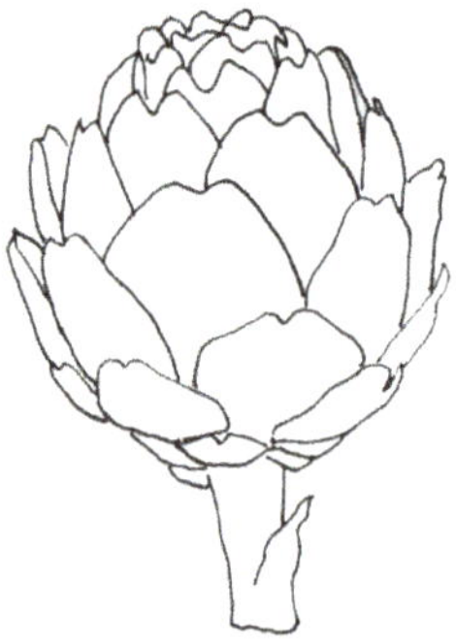 Vegetable: _____	 Vegetable: _____	 Vegetable: _____
Plant part: _____	Plant part: _____	Plant part: _____
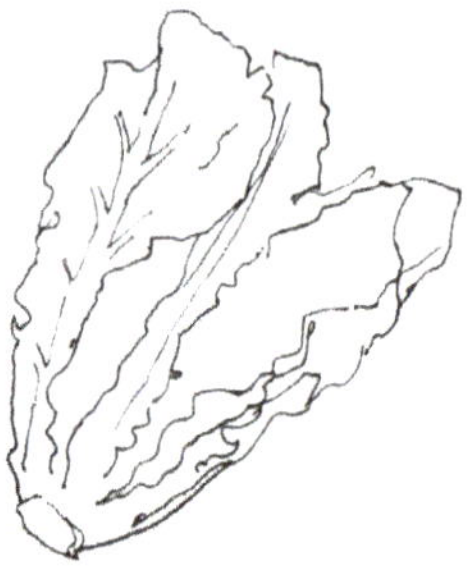 Vegetable: _____	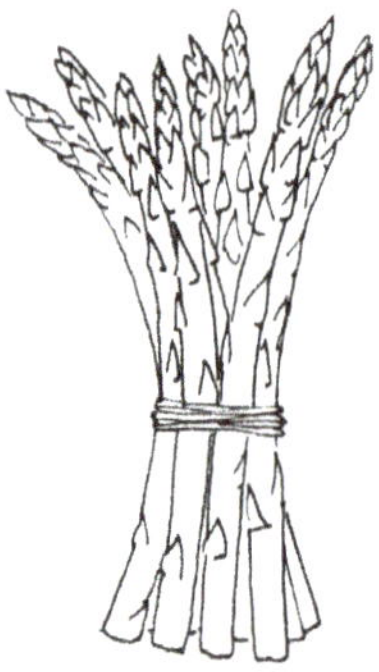 Vegetable: _____	 Vegetable: _____
Plant part: _____	Plant part: _____	Plant part: _____

Science in a Garden by Ross Mars | Reproducible

Activity

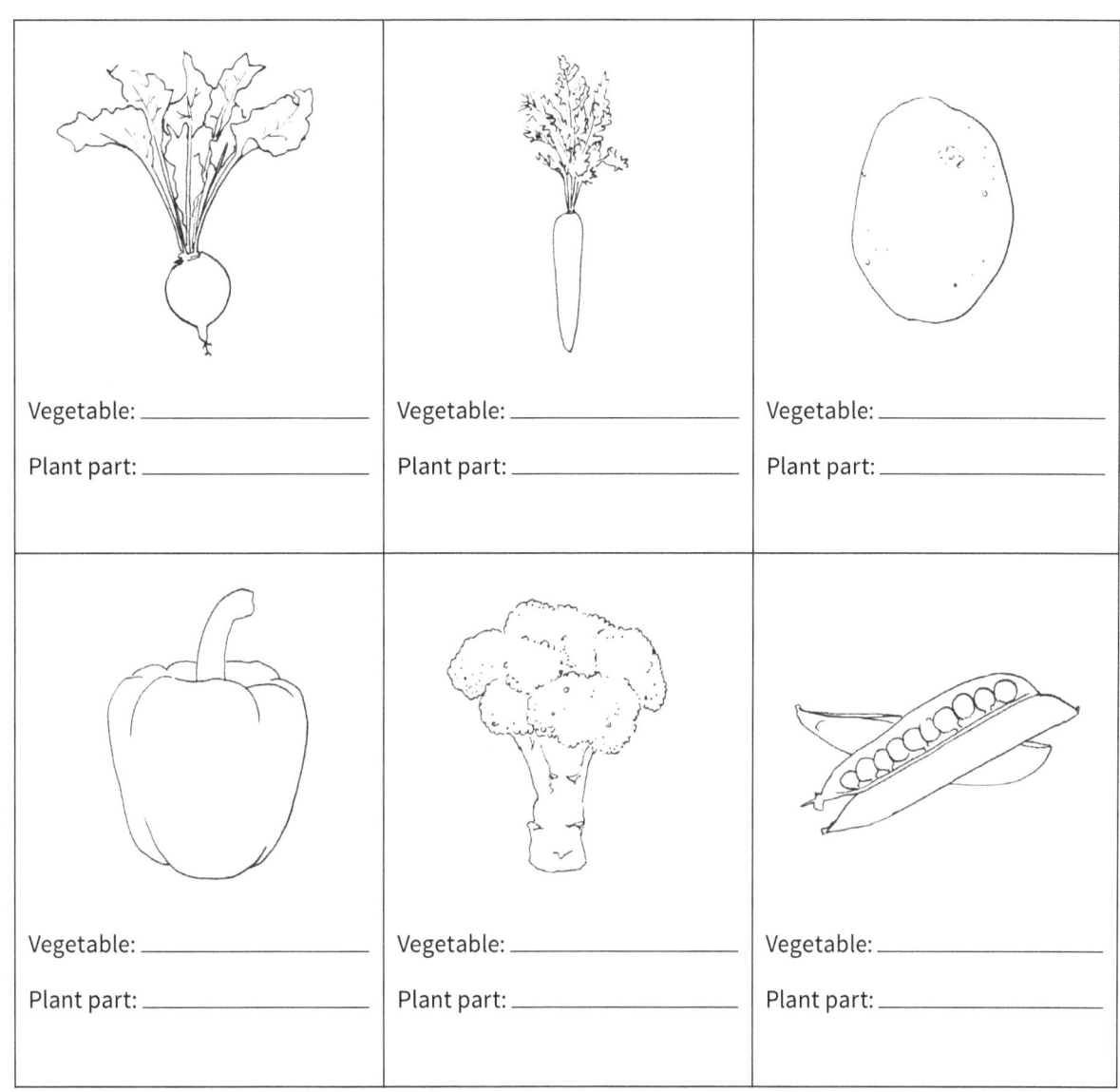

Extension

Cut a cross-section of the vegetables discussed above (or other seasonal vegetables that you have access to) to examine them. Attempt to identify what the vegetable is before working through and labelling them.

You might discuss the vegetables and how they have grown. Does the outside look similar or different to the inside? How might the insides have affected the shape, colour or size of the vegetable? Do they appear to have a high water content, or are they quite starchy?

You may also observe differences and similarities between the cross-sections. What might these tell us about certain vegetables?

Science in a Garden by Ross Mars | Reproducible

Activity

Construct a food pyramid

There are many different types of food, each with its own unique nutritional make up. The foods we grow in our gardens, our fruits and vegetables, are very good for us and give us the nutrients we need to function well. However, not all food is grown in the garden, and there are some types of food that we might want to enjoy less frequently as part of a balanced diet.

Guidance for how much of each type of food we should eat is often presented in a food pyramid but may be presented in another shape or form. Conduct an internet search to find as many different food pyramids or nutritional guidance images as you can. How are they similar? How are they different?

Based on what you learn about food pyramids and nutritional advice, cut out the pictures below of the common foods, from both the garden and the supermarket or restaurant, and make up your own food pyramid on a large sheet of paper.

Soft drink   Broccoli   Hot chips   Peas

Banana   Strawberry   Fish   Capsicum

Science in a Garden by Ross Mars | Reproducible

Cheese	Cake	Cherries	Wheat
Pumpkin	Potato	Eggs	Grapes

Extension

Vitamins and minerals investigation

Go into the garden and observe the foods you are growing. Research the vitamins and minerals common in these garden foods and compare them to one other. You might like to start a discussion with your group about healthy eating, vitamins, minerals and health benefits of the specific foods in the student garden.

Food groups

If the garden has a wide range of foods, you can observe the foods in the garden and then categorise them further into vegetable classifications or food pyramid classifications. Again, this focuses on the health benefits of food and a healthy diet while including the skills of observing and classifying.

Moulds

Moulds are easy to grow, but students should be very careful not to be directly exposed to them, as moulds can cause health issues. There are many different types of moulds. Some are useful such as the ones used to make penicillin, cheese and fermented foods, while others can cause plant diseases (sooty moulds) or health problems in humans.

There are two activities for learning about moulds. 'Growing mould' (p. 165) is a simple experiment that enables students to demonstrate that moisture and a food source are both required for mould growth. The bags are kept in a darkened space, but there does not need to be any discussion about the effect of sunlight on mould or its growth in a cooler place, such as a refrigerator. The effect of sunlight or lack of sunlight is the thrust of the second activity, 'What bread mould needs to grow' (p. 167).

The concept of a null hypothesis is introduced for this second activity. Normally students might write a hypothesis like 'Increasing the temperature will decrease (or increase) mould growth', but a null hypothesis simply states that temperature has no effect on mould growth. You shouldn't expect any difference in mould growth as the temperature is changed. Students are asked to discuss their experimental design and conduct the activity.

Moulds usually appear after a few days to a week. Most moulds are strands of filaments, called *hyphae*, which become interwoven patches known as *mycelium*. This can be seen as white fluffy threads on the surface of organisms or walls. Moulds reproduce by spores, and the spore capsules are visible to the naked eye as small black dots.

Once the activities have concluded, you will need to dispose of the bags or petri dishes. Often these things are incinerated, but wrapping the items in newspaper and disposing in the school bins is sufficient.

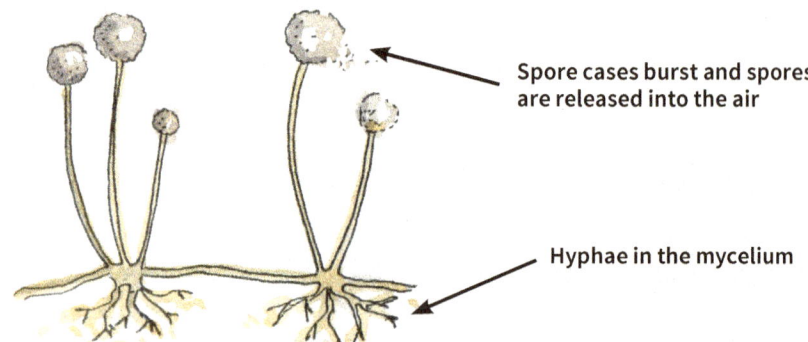

Spore cases burst and spores are released into the air

Hyphae in the mycelium

Growing mould

A mould is a type of fungus. It grows on living or dead things and feeds on them. Moulds are decomposers because they help to break down organic matter. Moulds prefer moist, dark conditions.

Materials

Bread

Tap water in a spray bottle

Fruit slices (apple or orange – about one-eighth of a fruit)

3 petri dishes (and lids) or zip lock plastic sandwich bags (resealable)

Hand lens or magnifying glass

Method

1. Lightly spray half a slice of bread. Spray once inside the plastic bag or petri dish. Place the bread into the bag or dish and seal. Label this sample.

2. Lightly spray one section of apple or orange. Make sure you have a slice that still has the peel on it. Spray once inside the plastic bag or petri dish. Place the fruit section into the bag or dish and seal. Label this sample.

3. In a third bag or petri dish place half a slice of bread. Do not spray this or the bag.

4. Place the bags in a cupboard or darkened space. Observe the bags over two weeks. Record your observations.

5. Use a hand lens or magnifying glass to observe the structures of the moulds. Do not open the bag or lid of the petri dish. There is a risk of disease or an allergic reaction because we do not know which moulds you have grown. Draw the structures you have observed.

Observations

_____
_____
_____
_____
_____

Investigation

Discussion

1. What is the purpose of the third bag?

2. What do you think would happen to the rate of mould growth if the bags were kept in a refrigerator?

Conclusions

Investigation

What bread mould needs to grow

Discuss with your group how you would design and perform an experiment that demonstrates that the amount of light has no effect on the growth of mould. List the materials you would require, your method, your predictions, your findings and conclusions.

Hypothesis

The hypothesis is: Light has no effect on the growth of bread mould.

This is called a null hypothesis.

The independent variable is: _____

The dependent variable is: _____

We need to control these variables:
_____

The control group will include:
_____

The experimental group will have:
_____

Materials

Method

Predictions

Investigation

Results

Conclusions

_____
_____
_____

Teacher notes

Yeast (Investigations 1 to 3)

Almost everyone eats fermented foods as part of their diet. Fermented foods include cheese, beer (also ciders, sparkling fruit drinks and ginger beer), black tea, soy sauce, yoghurt and vinegar.

Fermentation is basically anaerobic digestion primarily by bacteria and fungi (including yeasts), so removing air from an environment is essential for the process to occur. When microorganisms feed on the sugars in the foods they digest, alcohol, acetic acid (vinegar) and lactic acid (think sour milk) are produced, and all of these substances inhibit the growth and action of other (harmful) microorganisms. The fermented food becomes preserved food.

Every fermented product requires a specific microorganism culture. You have a choice with cultures: obtain a known (often store-bought) culture or let nature take its course (a 'wild ferment'), allowing a variety of bacteria and yeasts in the air to inoculate the mix.

There are three different activities students can undertake on the action of yeast as well as two yeast products that they can make in groups or as a whole-class endeavour. Investigations 1 and 2 are simple experiments on the action of yeast, while investigation 3 enables them to develop their own experiments.

169

Teacher notes

Notes for each activity

Investigation 1

You should expect little activity in cup 1, some activity in cup 2 and most activity in cup 3. The yeast in cup 2 works but at a slower rate. If some groups conduct the experiment by keeping yeast solutions in the dark, there may not be any significant difference, as yeast does not need light to work. Results should be the same for light or dark environments.

Investigation 2

Both bottles produce carbon dioxide gas, but you may find bottle 2 continues to produce gas due to the higher food (sugar) content available to the yeast cells. The balloon may be slightly larger. The balloons never get very big because the gas pressure is generally too low.

To demonstrate that the gas is carbon dioxide, you could grasp one of the larger balloons, remove it from the bottle and slowly release it over (from above) a lit candle. The flame should extinguish. Be careful not to blow the candle out with a rush of gas.

Investigation 3

You should lead and direct the discussion for investigation 3. There are many variables that can be altered in this activity. Students may be able to substitute baking powder for yeast, change the volume of yeast and sugars used to blow up balloons, change the temperature of the water, use thermometers to more accurately measure temperatures, use heated (killed) yeast or no yeast at all as possible controls, use a thermos flask (for some solutions) to better maintain constant fermentation temperatures, or add one tablespoon of salt to one of the yeast solutions (to inhibit yeast activity).

The class can make bread using bought yeast or make sourdough bread using wild fermentation. This is safe, but if you suspect fouling (noticeable by the colour and smell), carefully dispose of the product.

The addition of salt is an important step in many fermentation processes. The salt slows the rate of fermentation by yeasts and bacteria. Do not add it at the start of some recipes because you won't get the fermentation working. For sourdough, you add the salt to the dough to be baked but never to the starter.

Yeast 1: The action of yeast

Materials

Permanent marker

3 paper or plastic cups

Teaspoon

Yeast (dry or compressed yeast)

Measuring cups

Tap water (cold and warm)

Sugar

Optional: Aluminium foil

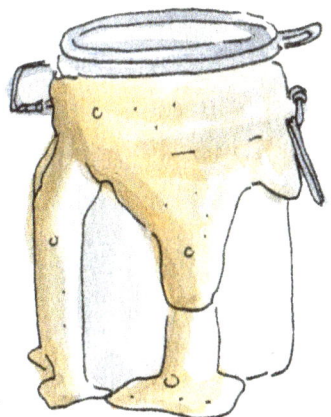

Method

1. Label the three cups 1 to 3.

2. In cup 1 mix one teaspoon of yeast (or 1 cm^3 compressed yeast) and half a cup of cold tap water.

3. In cup 2 mix one teaspoon of yeast (or 1 cm^3 of compressed yeast), one teaspoon of sugar and half a cup of cold tap water.

4. In cup 3 mix one teaspoon of yeast (or 1 cm^3 of compressed yeast), one teaspoon of sugar and half a cup of warm tap water. Your teacher will provide you with tap water that has been heated to 40°C.

5. Place your cups on a windowsill or classroom bench. Leave these for a few hours or even overnight.

6. Optional: Your teacher may ask some groups to cover the cups in aluminium foil – around the sides and over the top. This is to test the effect of light on the yeast. You can also place the cups in a cupboard.

7. Record your observations and explain the differences you observe in the cups. Draw some conclusions about yeast based on your observations.

Investigation

Results

Cup	Observations
1	
2	
3	

Explain the differences you observed in the activity of each cup (including any groups that kept the cups in the dark).

_____
_____
_____
_____
_____
_____

Conclusions

_____
_____
_____
_____
_____
_____
_____

Yeast 2: Measuring gas production by yeast

Materials

Labels

2 screw-top bottles or 600 mL soft drink bottles

Dessert spoon

Sugar

Measuring cups

Tap water (warm)

Yeast (dry or compressed yeast)

2 balloons

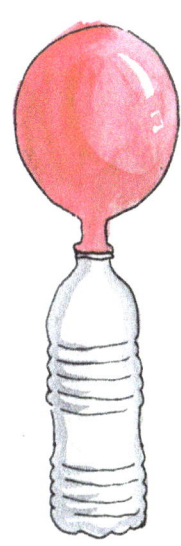

Method

1. Label the two bottles 1 and 2.

2. In bottle 1, mix one dessert spoon of sugar and a cup of warm tap water. Your teacher will provide you with tap water that has been heated to 40°C. Shake the bottle to dissolve the sugar. Add one dessert spoon of yeast (about one 7 g sachet) or 2 cm^3 of compressed yeast and shake the bottle to mix thoroughly – for about half a minute.

3. In bottle 2, mix two dessert spoons of sugar and one cup of warm tap water. Shake the bottle to dissolve the sugar. Add one dessert spoon of yeast (about one 7 g sachet) or 2 cm^3 of compressed yeast and shake for half a minute.

4. Place a balloon over the neck of each bottle. You may have to stretch the balloon a few times first by blowing it up and releasing the air inside.

5. Leave the bottles on a warm windowsill or classroom bench. Observe these for a few hours. Usually some reaction occurs within 10 to 15 minutes.

6. Feel the bottles, listen for sounds, smell any odours and notice any changes to the yeast solution or balloons.

7. Record your observations and explain the differences you observe in the bottles and size of balloons. Draw some conclusions about yeast based on your observations.

Investigation

Results

Bottle	Observations
1	
2	

Explain the differences you observed in the activity of each bottle.

_____
_____
_____
_____

Conclusions

_____
_____
_____
_____

Yeast 3: Factors affecting the action of yeast

Discuss with your group how you would design and perform an experiment testing the action of yeast. List the materials you would require, your method and your predictions. Perform the experiment and discuss your findings and conclusions.

Hypothesis

The hypothesis is: _____

The independent variable is: _____

The dependent variable is: _____

We need to control these variables:
_____

The control group will include:
_____

The experimental group will have:
_____

Materials

Method

Predictions

Investigation

Results

Conclusions

_____
_____
_____

Reflection

Discuss with your group how you could improve this activity or modify it to enable you to explore other ideas about yeast. You might have some ideas about the method you used or the materials you listed, or you could suggest better ways to measure yeast action.

_____
_____
_____
_____
_____
_____
_____

Make sourdough bread

Sourdough bread is fermented by wild yeasts in the air. You initially culture a starter, much like ginger beer, and then use this to make the loaf of bread.

Sourdough starter

Ingredients

300 g (2 cups) plain flour

> Note: This can be organic, white, wholemeal, gluten free, rye or a combination of these. The flour you choose is up to your preference, but fully wholemeal or rye loaves are quite heavy and don't rise as much, so it is best to mix these with equal parts white flour.

300 mL water

Equipment

Metric measurers

Mixing bowl

Tea towel

Method

1. Mix 100 g flour (⅔ cup) and 100 mL (⅓ cup) water in a bowl to make a sticky paste. Cover with a damp tea towel.

2. Leave on the kitchen bench for two days. (Check the tea towel – keep it moist.) The dough should look bubbly. If there are no bubbles, leave the mixture for another day or so before feeding it.

3. On days three and four, mix in 100 g flour and about 100 mL water to make a soft dough. It shouldn't be too runny, so add the water slowly and stop when it reaches the desired consistency. Cover and put aside. This is known as *feeding* the dough.

4. Divide the sourdough starter into two. You only need about 200 g starter (1⅓ cups) to make the bread; the other half is used as a starter for another loaf.

5. Place this new starter in the refrigerator and feed it every few days with a little flour and water to keep it alive if you are not going to make another loaf straight away.

Project

Sourdough bread

Ingredients

500 g (3⅓ cups) flour of your choice

1 tsp salt

200–300 mL water

200 g sourdough starter

Equipment

2 large mixing bowls

Teaspoon

Metric measurers

Tea towel

Baking tray

Knife

Method

1. Combine the flour and salt in a large bowl. In a separate bowl add a cup of water to the sourdough starter to make it runny.

2. Pour the sourdough mixture over the flour and mix by hand. Add water or flour as required to make soft dough – it should not be crumbly or sticky.

3. Knead the dough on a lightly floured bench or plastic kitchen mat for about 10 minutes. Flour your fingers and hands too and work the dough until you find that it is elastic (stretches without breaking).

Sourdough bread

4. Return the dough to the large bowl and cover once again with a damp tea towel. Let it rise overnight (it should double in size). The appearance of popping bubbles on the surface means it is more than ready for the next stage.

5. Use your knuckles to knead the dough once again. It will decrease in size. Place the dough back in the bowl, cover with the damp tea towel and let rise again over five or six hours.

6. Preheat your oven to 220°C. Turn the dough onto a baking tray. Gently shape it a little to make a cylinder and slash the top once or twice with a knife to vent any water as it cooks. Bake for about 30 minutes. Once ready, your bread should be firm and should sound hollow when tapped. Remove from the oven and turn onto a wire rack to allow the bread to cool.

Project

Make spelt bread

Spelt flour is made from the spelt grain *Triticum spelta*, a relative to common wheat *Triticum sativum*. It does have less gluten and more protein than wheat but is a lower-yielding crop with tough husks around the seed that makes it more difficult to harvest. Some people classify spelt as a subspecies of wheat because they are so similar in many ways.

This is a fermented food that is easy to make. You can use plain wheat flour if spelt flour is unavailable, and you can use all spelt flour in this recipe if you prefer – it will result in slightly coarser bread. The bread is delicious fresh as well as toasted. Add your desired toppings and enjoy!

Ingredients

2 cups organic spelt flour

2 cups organic plain flour

4 tsp dried yeast

2 tsp salt

3 tsp raw sugar (or 2 tsp honey)

2 tbsp light olive oil (or similar vegetable oil)

1–2 cups warm water

Equipment

Large mixing bowl

Tea towel

Bread loaf tin

Teaspoons and tablespoons

Measuring cups

Spelt bread

Project

Method

1. In a large bowl, mix the flours, yeast, salt and sugar. Make a well in the centre and pour in the oil and some of the water. Mix to a soft dough. (You may need less than a cup of water. Add the water slowly and only add what you need.)

2. Cover with a tea towel and leave to rise for about one hour or until approximately doubled in size. At this stage, you can take the dough to the following step or just turn it over with a spoon and let it rise again.

3. When ready, turn the dough out onto a lightly floured surface and knead until smooth. Shape into two equal dough balls and place side-by-side in the tin. Cover the dough with a tea towel and allow to rise almost to the top of the tin.

4. Bake at 200°C for 40 to 45 minutes until well-risen, golden and the loaf sounds hollow when tapped with the knuckles. Turn out onto a wire rack to cool.

Gluten

In this investigation, you will examine the presence of gluten in wheat flour.

Materials

Measuring cup

Wheat flour

Bowl

Water

Method

1. Add one cup of wheat flour in a bowl. Add water (½ to ¾ cup) and mix together to make a rubbery ball of dough.

2. Hold the ball in both hands and carefully run water over this ball, trying to hold as much flour as you can but allowing the starchy part to wash down the sink. Use your hands to pull the ball apart as it is being washed.

3. After a while you end will up with a sticky mass of gluten strands.

4. You could place this gluten ball in the oven and cook for 15 minutes. You should notice that the gluten ball has hardened. This is edible.

Extension

- Research gluten and its uses in cooking. What properties does the gluten bring to the mixture?

- Research the grains that have gluten in them. Research the variety of foods that have gluten in them. Are there any that surprise you?

- Research coeliac disease, finding out what problems it causes to human health and what symptoms are shown by sufferers.

- Research gluten sensitivity. What symptoms are shown?

- Besides gluten, what other food allergies are common?

Project

Make gluten-free bread

Gluten is a protein found in many cereals, such as wheat, rye and barley, and so can be found in most types of breads, cakes and pasta. Gluten-free grains include rice, corn, millet and chia. Most vegetables, fruits and meats do not contain gluten.

Gluten holds the bread together as it rises and prevents cookies and crackers from crumbling. Gluten is harmless for most people but may cause problems for a small proportion of the population who experience coeliac disease or a gluten sensitivity. Some people choose to eat gluten-free foods in the belief that they are heathier, but this may not be the case.

This activity is also dairy free, as milk and butter are not used. Instead, olive oil is used to provide some flavour and to make the bread more pliable. Eggs do not contain gluten.

Ingredients

1¼ cups lukewarm water

¼ cup (3 tbsp) honey

1 sachet (2 tsp) dry yeast

3 cups gluten-free flour (If you use self-raising flour do not add the baking powder.)

1 tsp baking powder

¼ cup (3 tbsp) olive oil

1 tsp apple cider vinegar (or plain vinegar)

2 eggs

1 tsp salt

> Note: If your flour does not contain xanthan gum, you may need to add 1 teaspoon. Look for additive number 415. Xanthan gum provides stickiness and thickens the mixture in much the same way that is achieved by gluten. Xanthan gum can be bought from most food stores.

Equipment

Mixing bowl

Metric measurers

Teaspoons and tablespoons

Wooden spoon

Measuring cups

Bread loaf tin or cake tin with tall sides

Tea towel or cling wrap

Project

Method

1. Combine the lukewarm water, honey and yeast in the mixing bowl. Stir to dissolve some of the honey. Set aside for half an hour to allow the yeast to activate. You may see small bubbles as evidence that the yeast is alive.

2. Add all the other ingredients to the bowl and mix well with a wooden spoon. You need a dough that is not too sticky but not dry either. Add more water to suit.

 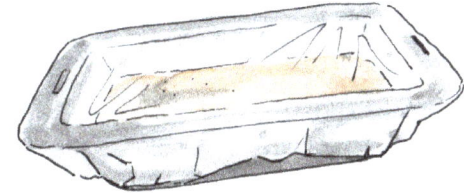

3. Scrape dough into a loaf tin that has olive oil wiped over all sides. Cover with cling wrap or a tea towel and leave to rise on a window sill or in other warm place but not in direct bright sunlight. The dough should increase from 50% to 100%. This may take an hour or so.

4. Preheat oven at 190°C at least 10 minutes before placing the loaf in. Cook for 30 to 35 minutes or until the crust is brown.

5. Remove the bread from the oven and allow to cool for 10 minutes before turning the loaf out onto a clean surface or wire rack.

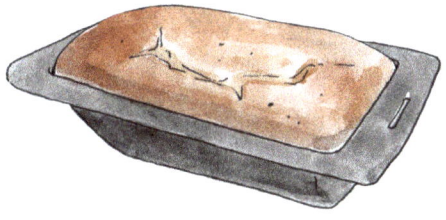 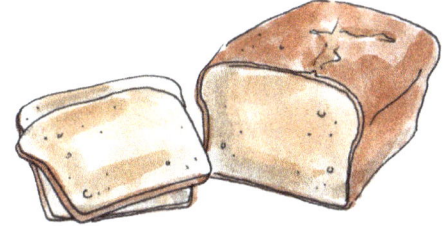

Discussion

1. Slice the bread and taste. What were you expecting? Is it a bread that you could eat if required? How different does it taste to other breads you most often eat?

2. Are you gluten intolerant, or do you know someone who is? Discuss this you're your group. How can you help a person feel included at special events, such as birthday parties and family barbeques?

Make damper bread

Many First Australians groups have traditionally used grinding stones to crush the seeds of certain plants to make flour. The flour is mixed with water to make seed cakes, which are then cooked on a fire.

The type of seeds or plant parts used depends on what grows in an area. For example, in central desert lands, the seeds of spinifex (*Triodia spp.*) and some wattles (e.g. elegant wattle – *Acacia victoriae*) are most common, while in Queensland the seeds of Bunya pines are used. In the Northern Territory, there are the seeds of water lilies, and in southern Western Australia you will find the seeds of wattles, such as the golden wreath (*Acacia saligna*), jam wattle (*Acacia acuminata*) and mulga (*Acacia aneura*). Wattles such as the elegant wattle and mulga are found throughout Australia, while jam wattles spread throughout the middle of Australia from central Western Australia through South Australia and into New South Wales.

To make enough flour for this recipe, you would need several kilograms of seed and a lot of effort. Most of the wattle seeds are very hard, and you would have to separate the chaff and seed coat fragments from the flour. In this activity, you will use common self-raising flour to represent the traditional flour made from ground seed. The project is designed to be completed in pairs.

Ingredients

1 cup self-raising flour

¼ tsp salt

1 tbsp (25 g) butter

¾ cup milk or water

Optional: 1 tsp sugar (for a sweet damper) or 1 tbsp grated cheese, chives or parsley (for savoury damper)

Equipment

Mixing bowl

Measuring cups

Teaspoons and tablespoons

Skewer or clean dry stick (for campfire cooking)

Baking tray

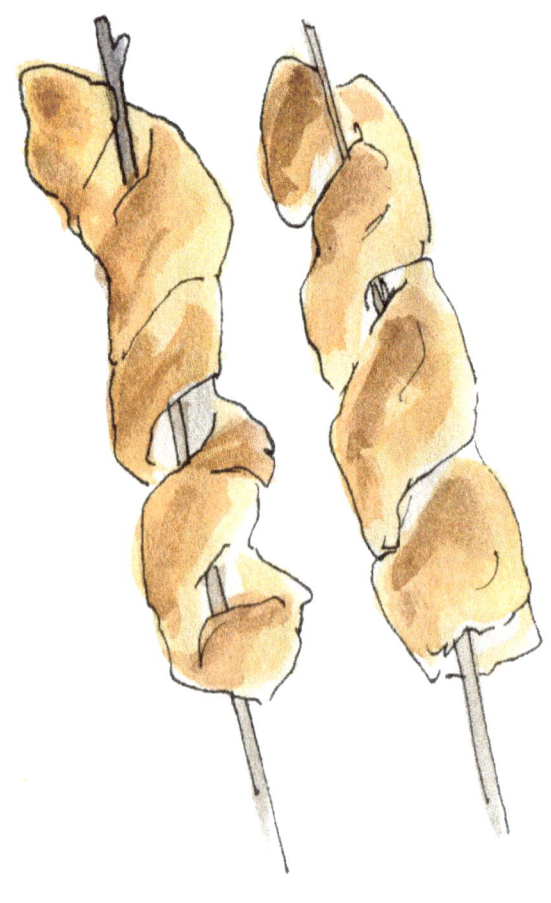

Project

Method

1. Ensure you have clean, dry hands.

2. Mix the flour and salt (and sugar or cheese as required) in a bowl.

3. Use your fingertips to rub the butter into the flour until the mixture looks like breadcrumbs.

4. Add the milk or water, a little at a time, and mix into a soft (not sticky) dough with your fingers.

5. Divide the dough in two (one for each partner).

6. There are two options to cook:

    (a) Roll the dough into a long, thin, flat shape. Wrap it around a stick or skewer (like a kebab stick). Cook by holding the stick over a campfire for 10 to 15 minutes. Rotate the stick to ensure even cooking.

    (b) Roll the dough into a ball. Use the palm of your hand to flatten the dough into a patty. Cook in an oven at 190°C for 20 to 30 minutes. The damper should be golden brown.

7. Cut the damper in half and spread your favourite topping on each side.

Background

Simple products to make from milk

The recipes that follow are easy to make and good fun. They highlight how we can reduce waste not just in the garden but also in the pantry.

Some information before you start

Before you get started, read the information provided about the equipment and materials you will use making your products from milk.

Temperature

Some cultures can work at room temperature, but many require temperatures similar to or slightly higher than our body temperature (these cultures thrive between 37 and 45 degrees Celsius), so it is crucial that you maintain a reasonably constant temperature during the fermentation process. You can do this by using a water bath, large thermostat-controlled pot or urn, a haybox cooker, thermos flask or something to keep your culture warm.

You also need to obtain a milk or beverage thermometer (not mercury or alcohol types). Digital thermometers are preferred, but analogue types tend to be cheaper.

Jars and bottles

A selection of different sized jars, with seals, will make your job a lot easier. Mason and Kilner® jars (wide mouth with screw lids), storage jars (clip top with rubber seal), plastic (PET) bottles and swing-top bottles (with rubber Grolsch seal) are all required to preserve your products.

Cultures

Every fermented product requires a specific microorganism culture. You have a choice with cultures: either obtain a known (mostly bought) culture or let nature take its course (a wild ferment) where a variety of bacteria and yeasts in the air inoculate the mix.

Sundry equipment

You will also need cheesecloth, muslin and a balance or scales. Muslin and cheesecloth are both fine cotton cloths (but do come in various mesh sizes), but any fine woven cotton material will work – even a tea towel.

Hygiene

Cleanliness, at all times, is essential. See page 159 to remind yourself of good hygiene principles.

Food products from milk

Milk is made up of a protein part, which separates into *curds*, and a watery part, which is the *whey*. The whey contains water-soluble minerals, lactose, proteins and many beneficial microorganisms that can be used to 'seed' other cultures when fermenting vegetables and beverages.

Most of the proteins in milk are known as *casein proteins*. Curds form when lactic (or other) acid causes the casein proteins to coagulate (curdle) together.

Yoghurt

Fermented dairy products can be easier for us to digest because the sugar (lactose) has already been broken down, and the complex protein casein has also been broken down into amino acids.

Ingredients

1 L milk

1 tbsp plain yoghurt culture (must be live culture)

Equipment

Metric measurer

Tablespoons

Milk thermometer

Thermos

Method

1. Heat milk to about 40 to 45°C. (If you think the milk may be contaminated, heat to 80 to 85°C to pasteurise it, but let it cool to 40°C again.)
2. Add the yoghurt culture and stir to combine.
3. Keep the mix warm by placing it in a thermos flask or wrapping it in something to insulate the mix.
4. Test the mix after six to nine hours. The longer you leave it, the sourer it gets. Once you are happy with the flavour, keep the yoghurt in the refrigerator.

Heating the milk is important to denature the proteins. This stops the yoghurt from staying lumpy.

If you want to thicken the yoghurt, strain the mix through a cheesecloth. You can either keep or discard the whey that you have removed from the yogurt – there are many uses for it as well! To flavour the yoghurt, add chopped fruit, honey or vanilla once the yoghurt is made and just before you eat.

Project

Soft cheese from yoghurt

Ingredients

1 kg plain yoghurt (must contain live cultures)

½ tsp salt

Flavouring: ½ tsp finely chopped rosemary, basil leaves, lemon zest or ground black pepper

Equipment

Metric measurer

Teaspoons

Mixing bowls

Muslin or cheesecloth

Method

1. Mix the ingredients together in a bowl.

2. Spoon the mix into a double layer of muslin or cheesecloth. Tie the cloth into a ball with string and suspend over a large bowl in the refrigerator or a very cool place for two days. The whey should drip out into the bowl and can be used elsewhere or discarded.

3. Remove the solids and roll to small balls. These can be eaten as required, although in many cases the cheese is similar in consistency to cream cheese. If kept in a refrigerator, the cheese balls should last a couple of weeks.

Soft cheese from milk

Ingredients

1 L milk

2 tbsp vinegar (lemon juice or 1 tbsp rennet will also work)

Optional: pinch of salt

Equipment

Metric measurer

Tablespoon

Saucepan

Wooden spoon

Muslin or cheesecloth

Mixing bowls

Optional: Shallow dish, wooden block

Method

1. Heat the milk to about 40°C (or 80°C if you are using raw or unpasteurised milk) in a saucepan, constantly stirring with a wooden spoon so the milk doesn't scald.

2. Add the vinegar and mix thoroughly. This will turn the milk into curds (solid part) and whey (liquid part).

3. Allow the separated mixture to cool to room temperature and then pour the mixture through a muslin cloth. Squeeze the cloth to remove all the whey. You can add another tablespoon of vinegar to the whey to extract more curds that you can filter out.

4. Scrape the curds into a bowl. Add salt and gently stir to combine.

5. Place the curds in a refrigerator. Eat within three days, after which it will taste tangy and will be better suited for recipes that require cheese in cooking.

6. To make a block of cheese, wrap the cheese in a piece of muslin or cheesecloth, place in a shallow dish and then add a weight on top to flatten it (another dish, a block of wood). You need a shallow dish to contain the small amounts of whey that continue to be squeezed out. Leave the block in the refrigerator for a day, unwrap and cut into cubes.

Don't expect a large amount of cheese from your litre of milk. Ten to 12 litres of milk makes about 1 kilogram of cheese, so 1 litre makes less than 100 grams.

Investigation

Make your own plastic from milk

Milk contains a protein called *casein* (which is Latin for 'cheese'). This simple molecule can be changed to make a polymer – many casein molecules all joined together in long chains. When acid is added to milk, the casein molecules clump together in large lumps. The lumps (milk polymer) can be held and moulded into shapes. Squeezing the lumps together makes the plastic.

The method for making plastic is the same as that for making soft cheese but with a slight variation. The soft plastic that is produced does not set very hard because commercial operators soak the casein plastic in formaldehyde, and this causes hardening. Formaldehyde is carcinogenic, so do not attempt to do this – leave it to the professionals!

Materials

1 cup milk

1 tbsp vinegar or 1 tbsp lemon juice (or ½ tsp citric acid dissolved in 30 mL water)

Muslin cloth

Cup or jar

Paper towel

Optional: Saucepan

Method

1. Heat the milk to near boiling, either on a stove in a saucepan or in the microwave for one to two minutes. Stir in the vinegar or lemon juice. The curds should separate from the whey.

2. Place a muslin cloth over a cup or jar and pour in the mixture to filter out the whey. To make sure you have all the curds, add some more vinegar or lemon juice to the whey and see if any solids precipitate out. Filter again if required.

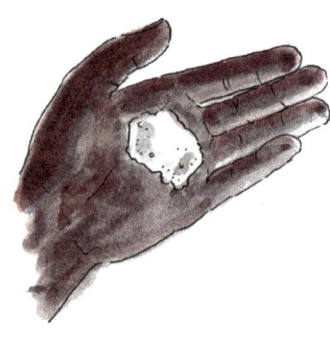

3. Lift the muslin from jar and squeeze any liquid out. Wash the acid out by pouring some tap water over the curds and allowing to drain over the sink. Squeeze the muslin again to remove any remaining liquid. Remove the curd mass from the muslin and wrap it in paper towel to further dry the soft plastic.

4. Mould the plastic into whatever shape you want. Allow to dry over a day or two. It should become rubbery and then harden a little, becoming brittle and even cracking.

Investigation

Make your own glues from milk

We have provided two simple recipes to show you how to make glue from milk. Use the instructions from 'Make your own plastic from milk' (p. 190) to prepare your curds.

Glue 1

To the curds, add a dessertspoon of bicarb soda. Mix well and reheat on the stove (or in the microwave for 30 seconds). Be careful – it will froth because carbon dioxide is made as the bicarb reacts with (neutralises) the vinegar or citric acid.

Remove from the heat when the curds are runny. Allow to cool a little, stirring to mix well. Test out the glue by sticking icy pole sticks or paper to paper or other objects.

Glue 2

To the curds, add a teaspoon of cloudy ammonia. Stir to dissolve the curds, which will make a milky paste – no need to reheat. Add more ammonia if you need to (a little bit at a time) but note that if you add too much, the glue becomes too runny. You want a thick paste.

Make your own honeycomb

Like milk, sugar, golden syrup, bicarb soda and honey are common in the kitchen pantry. They can be combined to make honeycomb, which is easy to make. However, if you overheat the mixture, it will end up being more like toffee than honeycomb. As the sugar solution heats up and the water boils away, the syrup changes consistency becoming progressively harder and more brittle (it is often called *crack syrup*). To test the consistency of the syrup, use a spoon to drop some syrup into a cup of water. Feel the honeycomb. It may be very soft and pliable, or it could be very brittle. For honeycomb you need somewhere in-between these extremes.

Ideally, a sugar thermometer is used to monitor the temperature as you heat the mixture. These are also called a *candy* or *deep fry thermometer*, which can measure temperatures up to about 200 degrees Celsius and can be bought from many kitchen supply stores. A milk thermometer is not suitable as the temperature of honeycomb production is well over 100 degrees Celsius.

This recipe is designed to be completed in groups of four or five.

Ingredients

3 tbsp (heaped) sugar (white, raw or caster)

1 tbsp honey

1 tbsp water

1 tbsp golden syrup

1 tsp bicarb soda

Optional: Shaved chocolate or chocolate bits

Equipment

Small saucepan

Teaspoon and tablespoon

Stirring spoon

Baking paper

Small metal tray or ceramic dessert bowl

Optional: Sugar thermometer

Project

Method

1. Combine the sugar, honey, water and golden syrup in a small saucepan. Place the pot over a low heat and stir occasionally to ensure the sugar has dissolved. This may take a few minutes.

2. Increase to a high heat and bring the mixture to the boil. Cook, without stirring, for five to seven minutes or until the syrup reaches about 150°C on a sugar thermometer. If the mixture smells burnt, you have gone too far. The mixture reduces as excess water evaporates away, leaving a syrup very high in sugar. Don't let the mixture bubble over the pot sides.

3. Remove from the heat and allow the bubbles to subside (this may take a minute or two).

4. Line a bowl or tray with baking paper.

5. Sprinkle the bicarb soda into the syrup and mix thoroughly. It will begin to change colour and foam a little as gas (carbon dioxide) is produced.

6. Carefully pour and scrape the mixture onto the baking paper. The syrup is extremely hot, so do not lick the spoon or use your fingers to wipe up honeycomb on the sides of the saucepan.

7. At this stage you could sprinkle some shredded chocolate over the mixture. It will melt quickly.

8. Once cooled, remove the honeycomb from the paper and break into pieces. Store in the refrigerator if required.

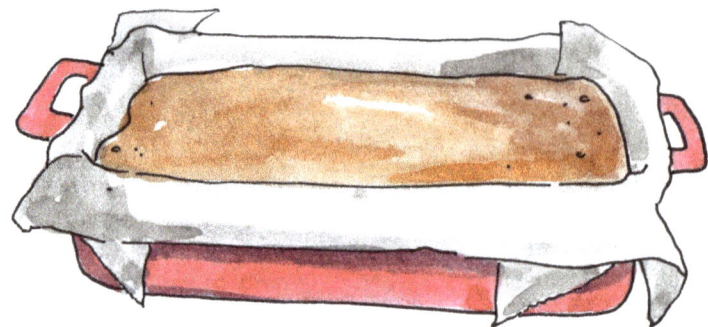

Observation and discussion

After observing the honeycomb process, discuss the following questions in your groups or as a class.

- How do the ingredients change during the process? What did you notice about these changes?
- What are the solids, liquids and gases in the process? Do these change or transform?
- Why do you think it is called honeycomb?

How does it work?

The syrup is made when the sugar dissolves in the liquid. The heat helps the water to evaporate, leaving behind the sugary syrup, which progressively becomes thicker as more water is removed. When the bicarb soda is added to the mixture, the heat of the syrup causes the soda to break down and release carbon dioxide gas. This gas gets trapped in the sugar and forms the bubbles in the honeycomb.

Herb sauces

Herbs are small plants with many different uses. They may have edible leaves, seeds or flowers; scented leaves for pest control; high levels of nutritious vitamins and minerals; aromas and flavour that add spice to other foods; and myriad uses for our health and wellbeing, such as essential oils.

Herbs are relatively easy to grow, and many home or school gardens will include common herbs. In the next sections, we will focus on those herbs that are often used in cooking and include some easy recipes for you to create with herbs from your garden.

You will most often use the leaves of the herbs in your cooking. It is the oils and other aromatic chemicals in the leaves of herbs that provide the seasoning and flavours to food. Some herbs, such as thyme and basil, add a mild sweet flavour, but the majority of herbs are either sour or bitter.

Basil pesto

Sweet basil is the common garden variety that is traditionally used in many tomato and meat dishes, and in making pesto. Basil leaves do have a fair amount of vitamin K but not much else. The herb is used fresh in cooking as drying destroys much of the flavour.

Many other varieties are used in cooking dishes and these include Thai, Greek and lemon basil. Most basil types are annuals (although in warmer climates basil may survive through winter) but you can buy a perennial basil, which can be regularly pruned, and the leaves used as required.

Ingredients

1½ cups fresh basil

2 garlic cloves

5 tbsp olive oil

Optional: ¼ cup pine nuts, ¾ cup parmesan

Sweet basil

Equipment

Mortar and pestle or food processor

Tablespoon

Measuring cups

Method

1. If you wish to add roasted pine nuts to your pesto, preheat the oven to 180°C and bake the nuts on a tray for five minutes or until nicely toasted. Keep a close eye on your nuts – they might burn when you're not looking!

2. Combine the basil and garlic (and pine nuts and parmesan if desired) with the mortar and pestle (or in the food processor) until finely chopped.

3. Gradually add the oil into the mixture and combine until smooth.

4. Store in an airtight container in the fridge. This pesto should last for five to seven days.

Oregano and garlic pesto

Common oregano is a small, perennial herb to 50 centimetres, although in colder climates it can die off in winter. Like bay leaves, the flavour of the dried leaves is strong. However, both fresh and dried leaves can be used in cooking.

High in fibre, calcium, iron and magnesium, oregano leaves also contain many organic compounds, which vary in concentration depending on the variety or cultivar grown.

Rich in organic compounds that give it its characteristic odour, garlic (along with most other alliums like onions and leeks) has traditionally been used for pest control as well as medicinal and culinary uses.

Garlic has a long growing season and is usually planted in autumn when the first rains arrive and then harvested in December or January.

Ingredients

1 cup oregano

2 garlic cloves (large)

½ cup olive oil

Optional: ½ cup parmesan, ½ cup almonds

Equipment

Mortar and pestle or food processor

Measuring cups

Oregano

Garlic

Method

1. Combine all ingredients (except the olive oil) with the mortar and pestle (or in the food processor) until finely chopped.

2. Gradually add the oil into the mixture and combine until smooth.

3. Store in an airtight container in the fridge. This pesto should last for five to seven days.

Herby tomato pasta sauce

Parsley is high in vitamins A, C and K and is a common garnish for salads, meat and potato dishes, and soups. The curly-leaf variety (*var. crispum*) is more decorative than the flat-leaf variety (Italian, *var. neapolitanum*), but both are easy to grow from seed. In cooler climates parsley may be biennial, but in warmer climates it tends to be an annual.

Curly-leaf parsley

Flat-leaf parsley or Italian parsley is larger than the common curly-leaf variety.

The tiny leaves of many thyme species are added as seasoning to omelettes or scrambled eggs and a variety of meats and sauces. Like rosemary, finely chopped or dried thyme leaves can be sprinkled onto bread or pizza dough to make a savoury loaf or base. For a mild citrus flavour, use lemon thyme (*Thymus citriodorus*). The leaves do not contain many nutrients but do contain an aromatic compound called *thymol* that is a good antiseptic and gives thyme its strong flavour.

Ingredients

1 tbsp olive oil

1 onion

2 garlic cloves

3 cups crushed or chopped tomatoes

½ cup basil

½ cup parsley

½ cup thyme

Thyme

Equipment

Cooking pot

Tablespoon

Measuring cups

Knife

Chopping board

Project

Method

1. Heat the olive oil in the pot over a medium heat.
2. Chop the onion and garlic and add them to the pot. Cook until the onion is soft.
3. Add in the tomatoes and stir the ingredients well to combine.
4. Simmer for 10 minutes to allow the sauce to thicken.
5. Stir through the herbs. You may wish to serve the sauce straight after adding the herbs to have a fresh taste or allow them to cook into the sauce for longer.

Rosemary and tomato pasta sauce

Until 2017, rosemary was known by the scientific name *Rosmarinus officinalis*, but now it is in the same group as other *Salvias*.

Rosemary is a woody, perennial herb with fragrant, evergreen, needle-like leaves and blue flowers. It is originally native to the Mediterranean region but is now common throughout the world.

Ingredients

1 tbsp olive oil

1 onion

3 garlic cloves

3 tsp rosemary

3 cups crushed or chopped tomatoes

Equipment

See page 197 for equipment list

Optional: Blender

Rosemary

Method

1. Heat the olive oil in the pot over a medium heat.
2. Chop the onion and garlic and add them to the pot. Cook until the onion gets a bit of colour.
3. Add the rosemary and cook for another minute.
4. Add the tomatoes and stir well to combine.
5. Cook on a medium heat until the sauce begins to boil. Turn the heat down to low and let it simmer for 20 minutes. If you have more time and want a stronger flavour, you may wish to let it simmer for up to an hour.
6. If you want a finer sauce, blend the mixture together before storing. Wait until the mixture is cool before placing in the blender – hot liquids and blenders do not mix!

Classroom cookbook

Gardens often produce large quantities of fruit and vegetables that we can't always use immediately. In this project, you will assess your garden produce, research appropriate recipes for these ingredients and create foods that can be stored or shared to avoid food waste. This project could be completed seasonally, and the researched recipes could be collected into a classroom cookbook.

1. What is in abundance in your garden?

2. Research recipes that include these ingredients. What recipes would use the most of your ingredients?

3. Select a recipe from among the ones you found to make. Why did you choose this recipe?

4. How would the end product need to be stored? (For example, if you make a jam it may be stored in a jar.)

Evaluation

Once you have made your chosen recipe, evaluate it. Is there anything you could do differently or change? Did the combination of ingredients work? Did you learn anything about what happens to certain foods through this recipe?

Make any alterations to your recipe, and then write it down to share with other students or classes. You may wish to share any useful tips that you learned during this process too.

Make your own hand sanitiser spray

An effective hand sanitiser needs to have a solution of at least 60 per cent alcohol. You can buy 70 per cent (or higher) isopropyl alcohol (rubbing alcohol) from pharmacies and scientific supply stores. Methylated spirts will also work in this project, and it has an ethanol content of 90 per cent. If you only have 70 per cent rubbing alcohol, don't use as much aloe vera gel or essential oil.

Aloe vera has a long history as a treatment for sunburn and itchy skin, so this spray can also be used in those situations.

To use the hand sanitiser properly, make sure your hands are clean (wash first if necessary), spray onto your skin and rub it in until your hands or skin is dry. You could spray onto one hand palm and then rub your hands together for half a minute or more. The longer you rub, the more bacteria will be killed.

Too much aloe vera gel will make your hands sticky, and the glycerol is essential as it is a moisturising agent and will stop the skin from drying out (from the alcohol). In commercial (hospital grade) sanitiser, hydrogen peroxide is also added, but this is unnecessary here.

Materials

Aloe vera plant (or store-bought gel)

Knife

Bowl

Blender or beater

Isopropyl alcohol (90% or more), or another alcohol

Glycerol (glycerine)

Tea tree oil (or eucalyptus, lavender or peppermint oil)

> Note: A few drops for each student or group – maybe 5 mL will be enough for the whole class. This is just to help mask the smell of the alcohols, although tea tree oil is also antibacterial.

Spray bottle

Method

1. Making aloe vera gel

If you are not using store-bought aloe vera, you must first extract the gel from the aloe vera leaf. A teacher will probably do this step for the class. Cut off the tip, edge and spines of the leaf. Slice the skin away from the gel and scrape out the gel. Place the gel in a bowl. Use a blender or egg beater to thoroughly mix the gel to ensure no lumps. Place in the refrigerator if you are not using it straight away.

Project

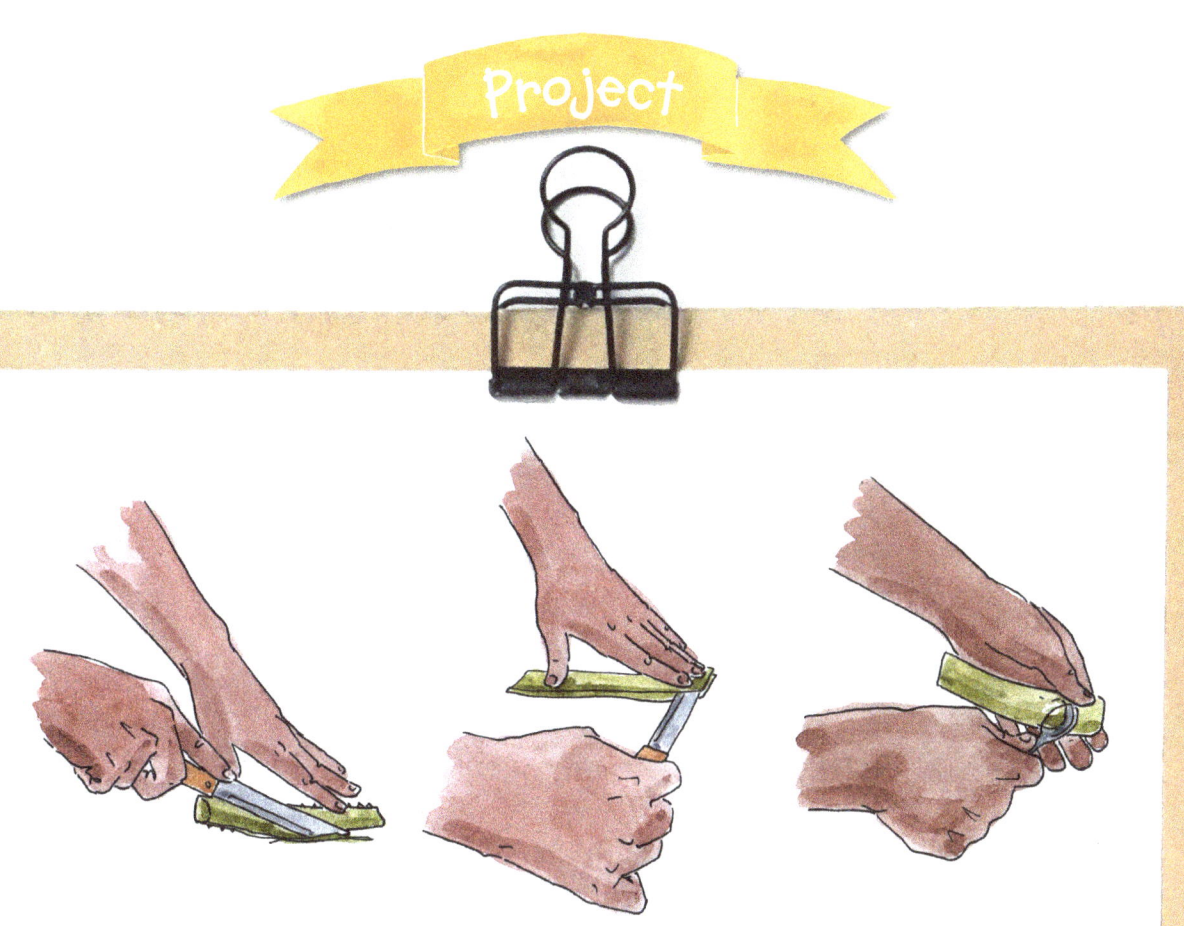

Cut off the tip, edges and spines. Slice the skin away (at least one side) from central gel slab. Scrape the gel out.

2. Recipe for spray

Mix eight parts alcohol with one part aloe vera gel and one part glycerol. Add a few drops of tea tree or other essential oil. If you still find some bulky aloe gel, you can strain the solution through a cheesecloth.

Project

Playdough garden decorations

Playdough is easy to make, and this project will show you how a number of common household substances can be combined to change into a new substance. The playdough can also be changed into decorations that you can use in the garden (i.e. for plant labels). The recipe that follows makes about a tennis ball-sized ball of playdough.

Materials

½ cup plain flour

½ cup water

1 tsp cream of tartar (potassium hydrogen tartrate)

2 tbsp table salt

1½ tsp vegetable oil (e.g. olive, sunflower) or baby oil (mineral oil)

Food colouring (a range of colours)

Saucepan

Wax-proof paper or baking paper

Resealable sandwich bags

Measuring cups

Teaspoons and tablespoons

Optional:

Skewer

Gas flame

Freezer

Thermochromic pigment

Rolling pin

Leaves, bark or sticks

Cookie cutters

Project

Method

1. Mix all ingredients (except the food colouring) in a small saucepan.

2. Stir in a few drops of food colouring.

3. Cook on a low heat, stirring continuously. The mixture will start to thicken.

4. Once the mixture is not fluid and loses its 'wet' look, remove the pot from the heat and scrape the contents onto a piece of grease-proof or baking paper.

5. Allow to cool and then knead the mixture.

6. Play! Make shapes. Swap colours with other class members. Use your playdough to make a model of a flowering plant or a common garden animal.

7. Keep your playdough in sandwich bag for storage. The salt you added is the preservative, so the playdough should keep for several weeks or even longer. Store in the refrigerator.

Changing the playdough

1. Roll two 1 to 2 cm balls of playdough.

2. Place one ball on a skewer. Heat over a flame until it is completely charred. Be careful not to light the skewer. Once cooled, break it apart. How does the inside feel compared to the outside shell?

3. Place the other ball in a freezer for a few hours or overnight. Remove. Is the playdough frozen solid or is it still pliable?

4. Use a pea-sized amount of a thermochromic pigment instead of food colouring. These can be bought online. These pigments change colour with temperature. Usually they are coloured when cold (air temperature) and become colourless when heated (by warm hands or temperatures above 33 to 35°C).

Project

Plant imprint labels

1. Roll out the playdough to 1 to 2 cm thickness.

2. Press leaves, bark or sticks from the garden into the playdough. Once you peel these away, they will leave a print behind on the playdough. What do you notice about the patterns in the playdough?

3. Using a cookie cutter, cut the playdough into shapes. If you don't have any cookie cutters, you could use a ruler to cut the playdough into rectangles to be plant labels in the garden.

4. Leave the playdough to dry out and harden over a few days, turning the ornaments over each day will speed up the process. You may wish to bake them instead.

5. Place the labels out in your garden.

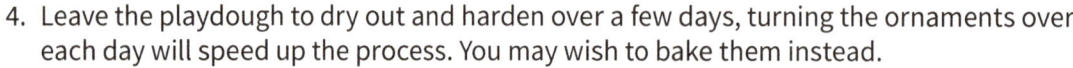

Extension

Observe the playdough ornaments in the garden across a week or more. Do you see any changes?

APPENDIX

Answers

Tools and their functions

	Size, shape and features	What is that tool used for?
 Tool: _____ Spade	Blade and handle in straight line Sharp square blade edge to cut soil	Cutting turf or soil lifting and removal
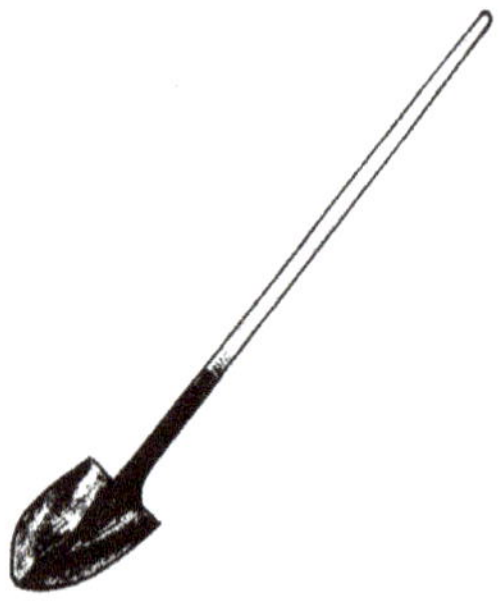 Tool: _____ Shovel	In this case a round mouth shovel Shovel blade at a slight angle Long handle	Scooping and shifting soil
 Tool: _____ Shears	Long cutting blades Tool about 600–700 mm long	Trimming grass, hedges and weeds
 Tool: _____ Metal rake	Sharp teeth Long handle	Enabling power to shift leaf litter and to level soil

(continued)

206

Answers

	Size, shape and features	What is that tool used for?
Tool: __Mulch fork__	Wide, many-pronged tool	Lifting and shifting coarse mulch and soil
Tool: __Lopper__	Long handles with robust blades	Trimming, cutting small branches
Tool: __Hand fork__	Hand-held tool with pointed prongs	Removing weeds and simple cultivation

Answers

Plant parts

Which part makes the fruit? FLOWER

Which part holds the plant and leaves upright? STEM

Which part absorbs water? ROOT

Which part contains seeds? FRUIT

Which part stores food underground? TUBER (also RHIZOME, CORM, BULB)

Answers

Stages of plant growth

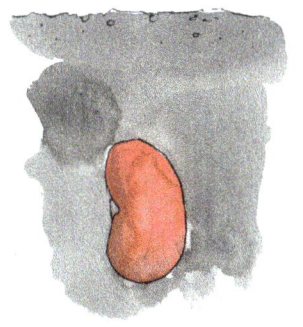
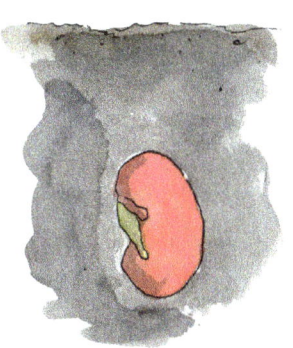
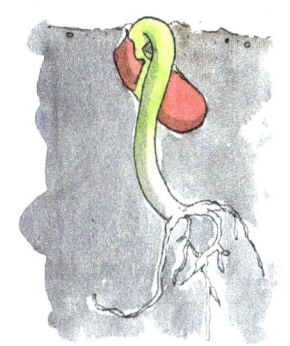

Answers

Needs and uses of animals

1. Animals have essential needs that have to be met if they are to survive. What are some of these?

    A. oxygen (air)

    B. water

    C. nutrition (food)

    D. shelter

    E. habitat

2. In what ways do animals differ from plants?

    - Animals can't make their own food. They need to find it.
    - Most animals possess sensory organs and rely on senses (sight, hearing, touch and so on) to examine their environment.
    - Animals can usually move more freely.

3. In what ways do plants differ from animals?

    - Plants generally do not move about.
    - Plant cells have thick cell walls (whereas animals have thin cell membranes), so they are upright.
    - Most plants use sunlight and photosynthesis to make their own food.
    - Plants use chemicals and special cells to detect light or communicate with each other (animals have sensory organs and a nervous system).

4. Both plants and animals are classified as living things. How do living things differ from non-living things? (What characteristics are common in all living things?)

All living things can respire, grow, produce wastes (excretion), move (even plants can make small movements of leaves, flowers), respond to their environment (organisms are sensitive to changes in the surrounding environment) and reproduce.

Answers

5. Animals have many functions in the environments where they live. They eat plants or other animals and some spread seeds from one area to another. Can you think of other functions that animals perform?

    Functions of animals include:

    - produce manure for fertiliser
    - pest control (e.g. ducks for snails)
    - till the soil (aerate, e.g. earthworms)
    - pollinate flowers
    - power to pull machines (cattle and horses)
    - fire control (e.g. sheep and other herbivores grazing weeds)
    - production of humus and soil (break down organic matter)
    - source of food for humans and other animals.

6. Humans also use animals to help make work easier. Horses can transport people and donkeys can carry goods over long distances. What are ways humans use animals to make work easier and save us energy and effort?

    - Horses can pull ploughs (till the ground) in the field.
    - Cattle or bullocks (male) can pull carts and wagons, or haul logs out of a forest.
    - Pigs are used to clear (dig out) rampant plants such as blackberry.
    - Chickens are used to clear up old vegetable gardens to prepare soil for next plantings.

How do these insects feed?

 Sponging	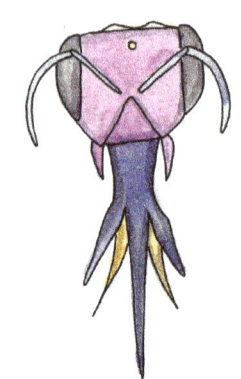 Chewing and lapping
 Piercing and sucking	 Biting and chewing
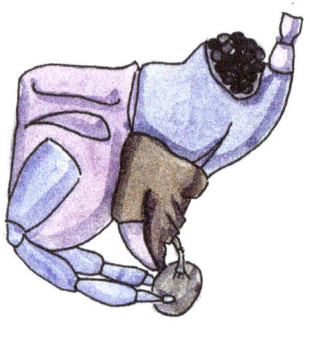 Rasping and sucking	 Siphoning

Pollination

1. What is meant by *pollination*?

    Pollination is the process of pollen (male cells) being transferred to the female part of a flower.

2. Examine these microscopic images of pollen grains and decide whether you think they are wind pollinated or animal pollinated. Place each letter labelling the pollen grain in the appropriate collumn.

Wind pollinated	Animal pollinated
B	A
C	D
F	E
G	H

    Some pollen grains are guesses as animals may eat the fruit and/or seeds and these are eventually passed out.

    G is willow which is mainly wind but also some insect

3. Explain the reasoning behind your choices in question 2.

    Animal pollinated flowers are usually some combination of large, coloured, nectar filled and perfumed to attract insects, birds and mammals.

4. Find and examine photographs of animals visiting flowers. What adaptations do these flowers have to attract pollinators such as bees, birds, small mammals and butterflies?

    Answers will vary.

5. Wind-pollenated flowers have different adaptations. What observations can you make about plants that use wind to transfer plants?

    Wind pollinated flowers are usually small, not coloured or perfumed, and have stamens above the rest of the flower so wind can catch and move pollen.

Answers

Adaptations in birds

Bird	Features of beak	Kinds of foods they might eat
Twenty-eight parrot	Hooked, crushing beak	Opening seed pods, seed
Chicken	Sharp pointed	Seed, insects
Black honeyeater	Long, narrow	Nectar
Spoonbill	Flat for filtering water	Aquatic animals
Sandpiper	Long, pointed	Small aquatic life in beach sand
Willy wagtail	Short, pointed	Insects and grubs
Brown falcon	Hooked for tearing	Meat (other animals, birds)
Goose	Blunt, thick	Grazing vegetation, seed
Red-browed finch	Thick, crushing beak	Seed

Soil critters

1. Which organisms are decomposers?

   Bacteria and fungi. It could be argued that earthworms are decomposers as they feed on organic matter too.

2. Which organisms are producers in most environments?

   Plants

3. What is the original source of energy for producers?

   Sun, sunlight

4. What role do termites play in the soil?

   They break down wood and dead plant matter.

5. The majority of organisms in the soil and compost are microscopic. What does this mean?

   They cannot be seen by the naked eye. You usually need a microscope to view.

Nutritional value of bush foods

1. What general comments can you make when the nutrient content of common figs is compared to sandpaper and desert figs?

   Sandpaper and desert figs are higher in energy and protein. They are similar in thiamine and vitamin C.

2. What general comments can you make when the nutrient content of the common tomato is compared to the desert tomato – the bush raisin?

   Bush raisin far exceeds the tomato in every category except vitamin C content, which is the same in both foods.

3. Comparing the sandpaper fig with the Kakadu plum, approximately how much more vitamin C is found in the Kakadu plum? Use the space below to show your calculations.

   Sandpaper fig = 234 mg/100 g.

   Kakadu plum = 3000 mg/100 g

   Comparison $\frac{3000}{234}$ = 12.8 (Kakadu nearly 13 times more vitamin C than sandpaper fig).

4. Of plum, quandong and sandalwood, which do you think has the overall highest nutrient value? Explain your answer.

   Generally, sandalwood has the highest nutrient valve. It is the highest in energy, protein, fat, carbohydrates, iron, magnesium and possibly vitamin C. Common plum is lowest in all categories.

5. Compare the data for pecan and macadamias. Pecan nut trees originate from North America while macadamia nut trees were originally found in northern New South Wales and Queensland. Which nut do you think has the highest nutrient value? Explain your answer.

   Macadamia nut has highest energy, fat, vitamin C, iron, magnesium and calcium, so it is most likely the highest nutrient valve. Pecan is only higher in protein (but not by very much).

6. Examine Tables 1 and 2 and compare all fruits and nuts listed. Why do you think nuts generally have a higher energy and nutrient content (such as protein, fats and some minerals) than fleshy fruits?

   The nuts are seeds and contain the most nutrients to enable a new plant to develop when it germinates.

7. What role does each of the following play in plant structure and function? You will have to undertake some research to find out about these substances.

   (a) Protein

   Proteins are made into enzymes and cell membranes. They also provide materials for developing new growth, including seed and fruit development.

   (b) Fat

   Fats are used as energy storage and are common in seeds and pollen. These can be broken down to release energy so the seed can germinate and a new plant can grow. Some fats are oils, which are common substances found in many leaves, fruits and seeds.

   (c) Carbohydrates

   Carbohydrates (mainly sugars) are the primary source of energy produced from respiration. These simple sugars are the building blocks for many other compounds found in plants such as starch, cellulose and sucrose (common table sugar).

Using food from the garden

1. What is meant by hygiene?

    Hygiene is the practices we undertake to maintain good health and prevent disease.

2. List a few examples of things you can do to maintain good hygiene.

    Maintaining good hygiene includes washing hands, using hand sanitisers, cleaning equipment, wearing protective clothing (gloves, overalls, boots), disinfecting surfaces and sweeping the floor (and generally cleaning up afterwards).

3. Explain, with a couple of examples, what safe handling procedures are.

    Safe handling procedures could include how we lift and shift produce and equipment as well as using protective wear when handling foodstuffs. For example, if we had to shift heavy boxes then we need to reduce any twisting, stooping and reaching, bend our legs and use them to lift, endeavour not to carry them a long distance or even get a helper to carry the heavy box together. Protective wear could include wearing gloves and aprons, so foodstuffs and produce are not contaminated by bacteria or dirt on your skin or clothes.

    Once our produce is picked we can take it to the kitchen. Often we need to store the produce for some time before we use it.

4. How can we prepare and store our food if we cannot use it straight away?

    Some produce needs preparation for storage. It might need to be washed, dried, smoked, pickled or salted. Foodstuffs can be stored loose in dry cupboards, frozen or kept in sealed containers in the refrigerator or pantry.

5. Imagine all the different types of food and produce we can harvest from the garden. List some of the ways we can use this produce.

    Produce can be:

    - eaten raw
    - cooked
    - made into other foodstuffs (e.g. fruit into jam, herbs for pizza topping)
    - dried and used for snacks (e.g. fruit leather)
    - frozen or put into storage to consume at another time
    - juiced (e.g. lemons and oranges).

Answers

Types of vegetables

Vegetable: Artichoke
Plant part: Flower

Vegetable: Cauliflower
Plant part: Flower

Vegetable: Onion
Plant part: Bulb (modified leaves)

Vegetable: Lettuce
Plant part: Leaves

Vegetable: Asparagus
Plant part: Stem (new shoots)

Vegetable: Spinach
Plant part: Leaves

Vegetable: Beetroot
Plant part: Root

Vegetable: Carrot
Plant part: Root

Vegetable: Potato
Plant part: Tuber

Vegetable: Capsicum
Plant part: Fruit

Vegetable: Broccoli
Plant part: Flower and stalk

Vegetable: Peas
Plant part: seeds and pod (dry fruit)

www.ingramcontent.com/pod-product-compliance
Lightning Source LLC
Chambersburg PA
CBHW042020090526
44591CB00023B/2921